Understanding the Tin Whistle

*With a Discussion on How to
Learn by Ear and Play From Memory
and
Suggested Drills for Rapid Advancement*

by Stuart Esson

For Frank,
and Ralph

"The best way to acquire a real knowledge of our folk music is to learn how to play it, and the easiest way to make a start is by taking up the whistle, which is the easiest instrument of all to play. All forms of ornamentation in use in rendering songs and dance music can be executed on it, and it costs only a few shillings."

Breandán Breathnach
Folk Music and Dances of Ireland

Table of Contents

Introduction	4
How to Use This Book	4
Choosing a Whistle	5
An Important Clue	5
The Fipple	5
The Body	6
Robert Clarke	6
Initiating Tones	7
Holding the Whistle	8
All About the Fingerings	8
Fingering Chart–Low Octave	10
Fingering Chart–Upper Octave	13
Octave Drill	13
Understanding C Natural	15
The G Scale	16
Practicing Scales	19
About the Modes	20
The Modes of D	20
D Modes Chart	23
The Modes of G	24
G Modes Chart	26
Shrill Notes and Sensitive Ears	27
Practice	27
The Learning Curve	29
A Most Beneficial Drill	29
The Music	30
Impressions on the Memory	31
Andy of Mayberry	32
What's in a Name?	33
Immersion	34
Let's Learn a Tune	35
Analytical Listening	36
Parts	39
Primes	41
The First Note	43
About Written Music	43
Developing Breathing Skills	45
About Learning Tunes from Notation	47
Putting it in Your Fingers	47
Ornamentation	48
The Slow Aire	50
The Sound Model	50
Rhythmic Variation	51
Melodic Variation	52
Appendix 1 — Strange Keys and Half-holing; Tunable Whistles	56
Appendix 2 — Hornpipes	57
Appendix 3 — Pointers on Notation	59
Appendix 4 — References and Recommended Reading	60
Appendix 5 — Furthering Your Musicianship and Sessions	61
Acknowledgements	63
About the Author	63

"It is a notable fact that musicians who learn by ear and play from memory have copious repertories, while those who learn from written or printed music are usually deficient in the memorizing faculty."

From:

Irish Minstrels and Musicians
by Francis O'Neill

Introduction

Books on learning the jigs and reels of Scotland and Ireland on the whistle seem to abound, but few go into much detail apart from showing which holes to cover and perhaps giving some 'pointers' or 'helpful hints,' but they are brief at best regarding the whistle itself and the myriad questions that will arise while becoming acquainted with the instrument. As well, none I've yet seen offer any real *program for rapid advancement*, nor is there much in the way of *discussion of the music and the skills employed in learning it*.

The point of my book is not to quickly show you how to play the whistle ("Here, cover these holes and blow! Here, have some sheet music!"), instead, I wish to show you how to learn the whistle quickly, by offering not only the necessary understanding of the instrument and the music, *but also a study program with specific drills for rapid advancement* as well as a thorough discussion of the music and the *mnemonic techniques for quickly building a large repertoire* of session tunes. That is the goal of this book: to get you what you need to rapidly become a competent whistle player.

But remember! The whistle, despite the simplicity of its appearance, is a serious musical instrument, commanding in tone, yet capable of intimate expression. In beginning the study of any such thing, the trick to learning quickly is at first to go slowly – to be patient and get your ground work done right; then you'll see how rapidly you can gain in ability, all for having been a little patient and disciplined.

How to Use This Book

The best use of this book will be to read it cover to cover, even as you begin to make your first tones. Though the learning curve is a step-by-step process and any written explanation must follow a somewhat lineal pattern, having the fullest possible knowledge of what is going on as you even begin is an immense asset, and a valuable part of my program for rapid advancement. My whistle teacher, very old fashioned, was often upset with me for "going ahead of her," but the more I understood about the whistle and about the music, the quicker my ability to play advanced! This would seem to be given, but then again, look at the dearth of detail in most whistle books! I am going to get into some close detail here, hopefully answering a lot of the questions and helping to resolve the problems that will invariably crop up as you begin your journey up the learning curve to solid musicianship on the tin whistle. Now, one point of this book is to discuss developing the skills for playing from memory – not to explain how to read sheet music, but instead how to understand and remember the melodies. Musical notation will be discussed only sparingly.

I have quite a lot to tell you before I even explain how you make your first tones, so let's get down to it!

Choosing a Whistle

Now, perhaps you already have a whistle. If not, most music stores that deal in traditional instruments should have some in supply. My advice is to go buy a cheap one in the key of D. The average cost of the average tin whistle (two of my favorite makers are Generation or Oak) is nowadays roughly ten dollars. Most any cheap whistle will get you started. The key of D is recommended as this is the key that agrees with most all of the other session instruments. You will notice that almost all, if not all, our tunes as performed in session playing will be in the keys of either D or G; and the D whistle can do both of these. I began with the much larger B flat whistle, just by happenstance. The different keys with their various sizes have different air speed requirements (much more on this later), but I don't think it makes any difference in someone's initial progress if they use a whistle other than the D.

An Important Clue

The key to quickly getting control of the whistle is in understanding the physics of the instrument, not only how it works, but why it sounds the way it does. An experienced player can make a tune sound smooth and eloquent, but to a beginner, getting even the first tones under control can seem pretty formidable. Understanding the raw mechanics will help you get past this initial hurdle. I don't want you to give up on it if at first you don't get the sound you expect. Whistles can be fussy little instruments: some play more easily than others, some you will get along with, and some will not want to cooperate very well. It has been my experience that the cost of a whistle has little to do with how well it will play. I've played some very expensive whistles that were just plain bad. Don't be fooled into thinking that getting an expensive whistle is the way to find a good one. *Getting some experience so you have a sense of what you are dealing with is the way to find a good one*, and most any off the shelf, loaner, or old hand-me-down will do fine for beginning to get whistles figured out.

The Fipple

Now, you'll see that the whistle has two parts: the mouthpiece (usually plastic), which is called the fipple; and the tube part, called the body. It is the fine points of *both* that have *everything* to do with how a whistle *will sound and perform*.

As we blow into the fipple, our breath is directed down a narrow slot and directly on to a sharp edge: the fipple 'blade,' which splits the air stream, causing it to vibrate as part of the air stream goes off the top and part goes down the tube. It is this vibrating stream of the air reflecting off the inside surface of the body that we hear as our tone. A comparison to a few other wind instruments will broaden our understanding of what this means to us.

The bagpipe, though a wind instrument, uses none of the human lung's capacity for expressive manipulation; rather, the air stream is blown into a bladder and further compressed into one steady stream (some bagpipes omit the lungs altogether and use bellows), which then activates the reeds of the chanter and drones, producing the tones we hear. Hence, the piper's vehicle of expression is in how he manipulates the steady, machine-like airstream in forming the tune: the tempo, rhythmic variations (by which I mean compressing or expanding time values within a steady beat framework), ornamenting with grace notes and slurs, melodic variations and anything else the piper can pull out of his bag of tricks, *but* nothing like expression via *direct breath articulation*.

The trumpet, on the other hand, with its mouthpiece to which tightly pursed lips apply direct lung pressure down a broadcasting tube, is at the other end of the spectrum in this regard. The sense of musical expression is in the manipulation not only of the melody but in the manipulation of the musician's air stream by *direct and dexterous lung power*.

The flute, with its simple sharp-edged oval hole that takes the breath and splits it (also called the fipple), is another instrument where the musician's direct airplay is a huge part of the vehicle of expression; as with the trumpet, a lot of skill is required of the lips. However, the fipple of the whistle, with its narrow slot and blade, has to be, mechanically speaking, the easiest of all; one need only blow into it and a tone is produced. It is primarily this feature that makes the whistle such an expressive instrument. It is also this feature that makes a beginner's lack of control leap out in high definition.

Don't let this dismay you. A smooth, controlled, musical sound will be yours; but experience alone will get it for you. It would be hard, if not impossible, to describe the subconscious processes involved; but basically your body intuits how to make the tones sound like you think they should, through the process of trial and error, over repeated experience, in much the same way we learned to make the tones we use to make our speech. Often, when a whistle doesn't perform well or has difficulty with certain tones, the problem is the fipple – maybe a nick or burr in the blade edge – but this kind of thing you can only determine after gaining some solid experience.

Width of blade has a lot to do with how fipples perform. Wider fipple blades demand a lot more air. However, too narrow, and the whistle will tend to chirp; that is, give off a high-end harmonic unexpectedly (this is also caused by blowing a little too hard). The balance is so delicate that even 1/16 of an inch makes a noticeable difference. But as I said earlier, most cheap store-bought (as opposed to custom made) whistles are adequate to begin getting these things figured out.

Now, to explain the other part…

The Body

I am sure you have noticed whistles come in a variety of sizes and are made of a variety of materials – some even conical rather than a straight tube. It is the distance from the fipple blade to tube end, relative to the tube's diameter, that determines the basic tone, or pitch, of your whistle. This works on the same principle as the church organ or the pan pipes. Now, the larger the whistle's body, the more breath it will take to play it. The B flat whistle, for instance, will require a much larger volume of breath than a smaller D whistle. Once again, the maker has a delicate ratio to balance here. You'll notice in most cases the longer the whistle, the larger the diameter of the body. A lot of whistle makers use a 7/16 inch diameter brass tube for the body of the D and the E flat whistles. This seems to be about the perfect length to diameter ratio. You see, getting your whistle to play a full two octave range, as any whistle should be able to manage, is as much about air speed as it is about fingering; and with too wide a body, you simply cannot accelerate the air stream enough to get the highest notes, blow hard as you will. So, correct design is very important.

You'll notice some whistles are conical. The Clarke Whistle, a wonderful little instrument, is conical. It could be said this really got started with the Clarke.

Robert Clarke

Legend has it that in 1843, an Irish farm hand living near Manchester, England began manufacturing whistles made of tin plating. After purported disagreements with his employer, he set out across the countryside with his whistles and equipment in a wheelbarrow, and a repertoire of 50 tunes. He began selling these new tin whistles for a penny; hence, the monikers, "Tin Whistle" and "Penny Whistle" (could any of these originals of Clarke's manufacture still exist?). It is my opinion that Mr. Clarke was a genius; whistles had formerly been made of wood, bone, even stone, but these more primitive whistles might not have much in common with what the whistle has become since Robert Clarke.

Now, the conical shape is all about air acceleration. You don't have to blow nearly as hard to accelerate the air speed in a conical tube as you do a straight tube; the design does it for you, just like water in a garden hose being forced through a narrow jet. Hence, the Clarke is a very easy whistle to play. It is usually very sweet and mellow of tone, though due to the primitive fipple, they demand a lot of air; and with the conical shape, it doesn't project its sound very well. It is kind of a quiet whistle, if there is such a thing. Experimenting with both types of body, conical and straight tube, will help you immensely in gaining an intuitive understanding of air speed as it relates to octave.

You'll notice the bodies of various whistles are made of different materials: folded sheet metal, plumbers' brass tubing, nickel-plated brass tubing, even PVC, and I am sure there are more. *Each surface will react differently to your air stream: sound differently, and play differently.* The thickness of the body's material also has a huge bearing on the sound and performance; for instance, a thick-walled, nickel-plated whistle will have a smooth but heavy sound. This thick, smooth, shiny sound is like the thick, smooth, shiny tube that produced it. A thin gauge, raw brass tube will have a rougher, drier, thinner, and scratchier tone, as the rough brass puts up much more resistance to your air stream and there is less density of the body to carry the vibration.

It has been my observation that a lot of whistlers start out with the nickel-plated brass, but in time, seem to favor the straight brass tube. They all have quite a different character. So as a beginner just starting out, don't be afraid to try a few different whistles. You'll like one more than the others at first. Stick with it for awhile. Later, once you have collected a fair amount of tunes, you'll find you prefer some tunes on certain whistles and others on different ones. Playing the various sizes and types rounds out your experience with the instrument and opens the imagination up to a broader spectrum of tonal qualities to make use of.

I should mention here that whistles do not like to play cold. Just like a cold chimney flue, they will put up resistance at first. Though they really take only a few bars to begin to warm up, some whistlers will cover the whole fipple with their mouth and, covering all the holes, blow a slow lungful of warm breath through to get their whistle primed.

Initiating Tones

So, on to how to play the whistle, which begins with how to make tones. Now, a lot of whistle books will instruct you to use a flute player's technique, called 'tonguing' to initiate tones, but that is a very bad recommendation. A better technique is what is called 'percussive breathing'. With tonguing, the tip of the tongue is placed lightly on the roof of the mouth just behind the front teeth and is dropped, or blown out of the way, as it were, to initiate the tone with a sudden strike of the air stream. This lends to a choppy, staccato effect, which is used heavily in some regional styles and is a great way to ornament a melody, with the occasional stark punctuation of chosen notes. But listen closely to good whistle players and you will notice that generally, they are playing long strings of notes and quavers (groups of notes) together in long, eloquent phrases, often very quickly. A breath is taken, and the next phrase begins (usually) without any sharp 'staccato' punctuation. This is accomplished with *percussive breathing*, which is to hit the fipple blade with a sharp push of air from a sudden constriction of the upper chest and throat (you will employ this in a moment when I introduce you to the scales). This begins the often long, steady though eloquently articulated air stream we play our phrases with. It strikes the first note of the phrase with clear definition yet stops short of the pronounced 'tuh' effect produced by tonguing.

Percussive breathing is developed as a habit quite naturally, just follow this simple suggestion: as a beginner, always keep your tongue out of the way! At most, the back of the tongue might rise up towards the back of the mouth as you manipulate your air stream (once you get a feel for such things, that is), but for now, always keep the tip of the tongue out of the action. Tonguing, as an ornamental technique, will fall into place easily and naturally when your playing has developed to the point where you're ready for it.

To put it into a brief phrase, you could say that, for the most part, we begin our tones with a 'huh,' not a 'tuh.'

Holding the Whistle

I should say something here about holding the whistle. You see, the whistle has six holes – three are to be covered with the index, middle, and ring fingers of the left hand, and three are to be covered in like fashion with the right hand, but I am not going to tell you which hand to use for which holes. If you are left-handed, you might be naturally drawn to using your right hand to cover the high three holes rather than the left (you will notice in pictures of the amazing whistler, Mary Bergin, that she has her right hand on the high holes). If this feels more natural to you, I am not going to say not to do it but I do want to point out that the fingerings for the tin whistle and the traditional flute are the very same. If you learn the whistle with the left hand on the higher three holes, the fingering patterns you learn are quite easily adapted to the traditional flute, should you ever wish to pick it up as well.

Take your whistle, place the index finger of your left hand over the top hole, the middle finger over the second hole, the ring finger over the third hole, and rest the thumb gently on the opposite side between the index and middle finger. We use the pad of our fingers, not the tip end. Place the index finger of the right hand over the fourth hole, the middle finger over the fifth hole, and the ring finger over the sixth hole. Rest the thumb gently on the opposite side between the index and middle fingers and rest the little finger on the body below the sixth hole. This gives your right thumb something to counter-push with in holding that is not constantly in motion. Some whistlers keep their low pinkie up while playing (the fact is, mine bobs up and down out of habits learned on the concert flute, reaching for levers that aren't there); but I think it helps in holding your whistle to try and keep it down.

Now, I keep saying 'gently' regarding the thumbs. This is because beginning players do tend to unconsciously grip the whistle too tightly, making movements of the fingers stiff and jerky. *Consciously relax your hands*, hold the whistle *lightly*, and keep reminding yourself of this until it becomes habit to have a relaxed, easy grip, and not automatically tense up the hands as is natural in gripping things.

All About the Fingerings

So, whistle in hand, fipple between lips (but not touching the teeth), and all holes covered, blow an *even, gentle stream* of breath through your whistle.

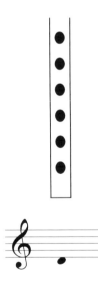

This will give you the whistle's lowest note, the low D, which fingering we'll diagram this way with its representation on the musical staff directly to the right.

Before you try anything else, I want you to try this experiment: covering all holes as for the low D, and filling your lungs comfortably full of air, blow a gentle stream of air for the low D note. Now, with the same breath, blow harder and harder still; blow as hard as you can, maintaining all holes covered. The note changed an octave, right? It probably went up another octave again, and you probably heard some other harmonics as well (you may have even broken a window somewhere close). This demonstrates how the volume, hence the speed, of your breath determines the octave and gives you a feel for how whistles work.

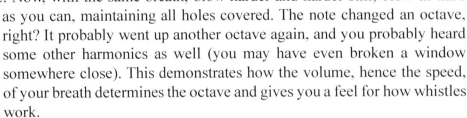

Now, while covering all holes and blowing a steady, even, low D note, pick up your right hand ring finger, uncovering the lowest hole for the note E.

Pick up the right hand middle finger, uncovering the second hole from the bottom, for the note F sharp (the D whistle, used here as the model, has two sharps in its key: C sharp and F sharp).

Pick up the right hand index finger and uncover the third hole, for the note G, which would be as illustrated here on the musical staff.

Now, keeping the little finger of the right hand on the whistle below the lowest hole (like I say, not required but a good habit to develop), pick up the ring finger of the left hand and uncover the fourth hole from the bottom for the note A.

Pick up the middle finger of the left hand and uncover the fifth hole for the note B.

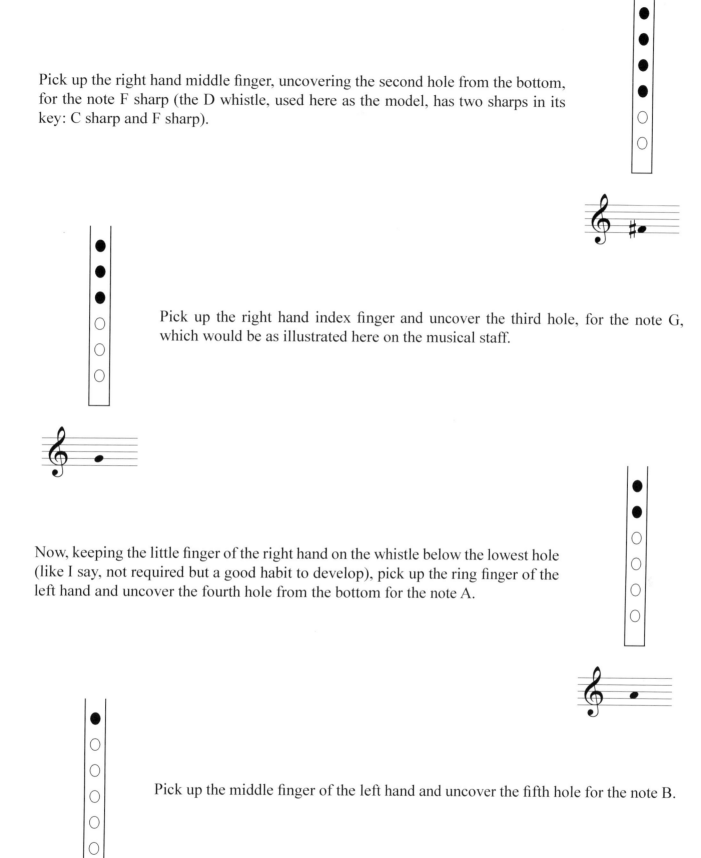

Now, pick up the index finger of the left hand (where is that right hand little finger?) and uncover all holes for the note C sharp.

You may not have noticed, but as the tones rose up the scale, your breath minutely increased in volume with each note; your body *intuitively increased the air flow to the correct level to make the tone sound full and strong.*

The next note brings us to the middle D note, one octave up from the lowest tone. For this note, cover all holes again as for the low D, but for the top hole, keep the left hand index finger up.

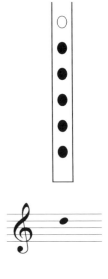

Though we know this note can be obtained by simply blowing harder with all holes covered, the whistle will make a middle D tone more easily with this top hole open.

So, all in a row, the fingering chart for the low octave looks like this:

Low D Octave

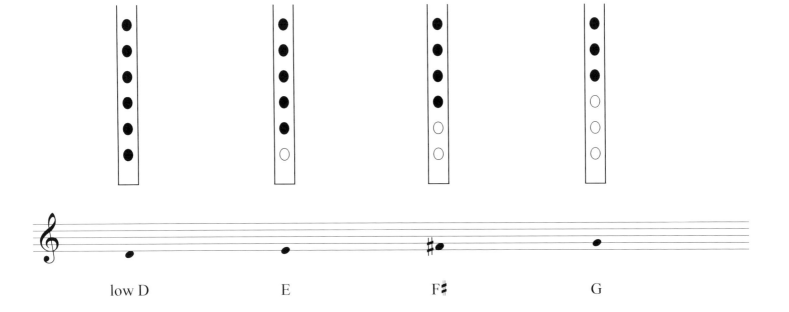

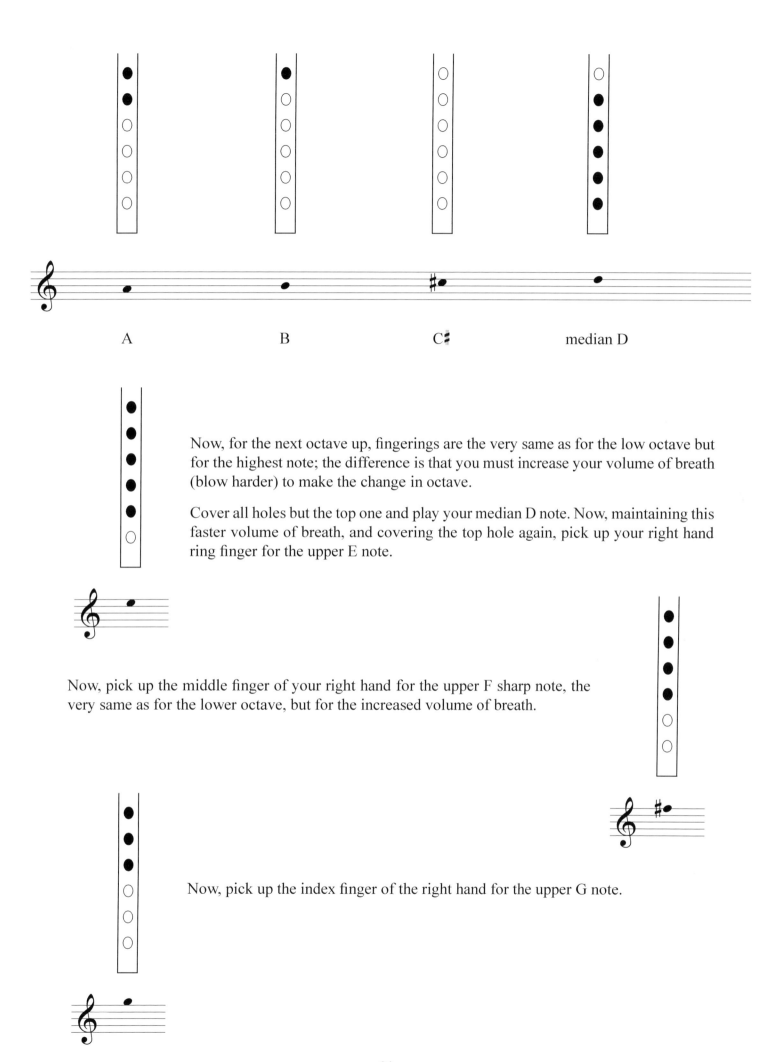

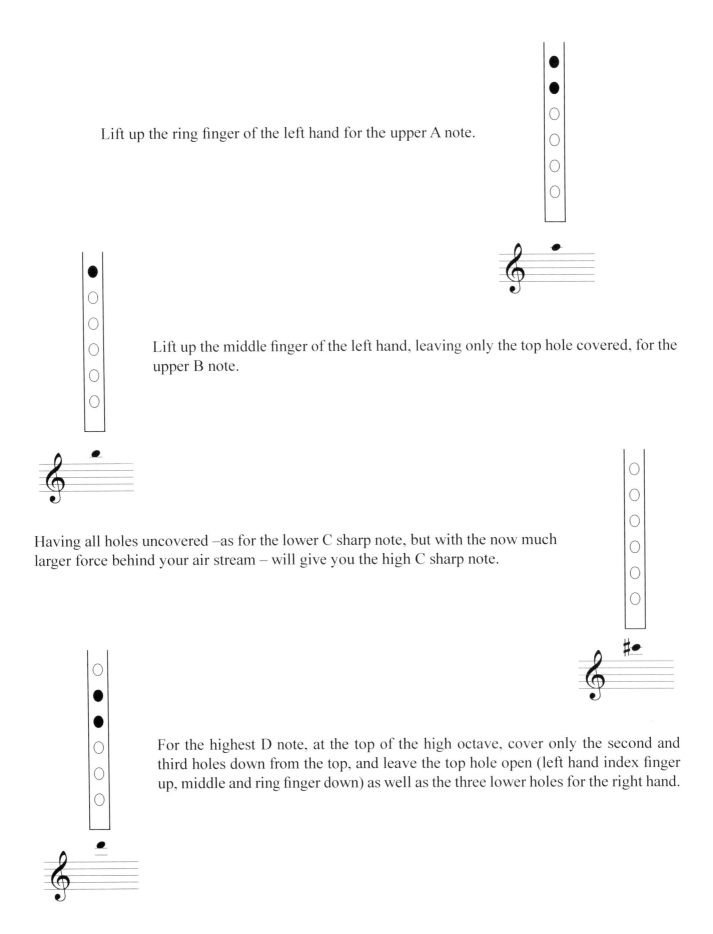

Lift up the ring finger of the left hand for the upper A note.

Lift up the middle finger of the left hand, leaving only the top hole covered, for the upper B note.

Having all holes uncovered –as for the lower C sharp note, but with the now much larger force behind your air stream – will give you the high C sharp note.

For the highest D note, at the top of the high octave, cover only the second and third holes down from the top, and leave the top hole open (left hand index finger up, middle and ring finger down) as well as the three lower holes for the right hand.

This will get you an adequate high D, though you can tell whistles don't necessarily like to go there; the note is usually quite shrill. I will later explain some drills for getting these high notes under control.

So, the fingering chart for the upper octave looks like this:

High D Octave

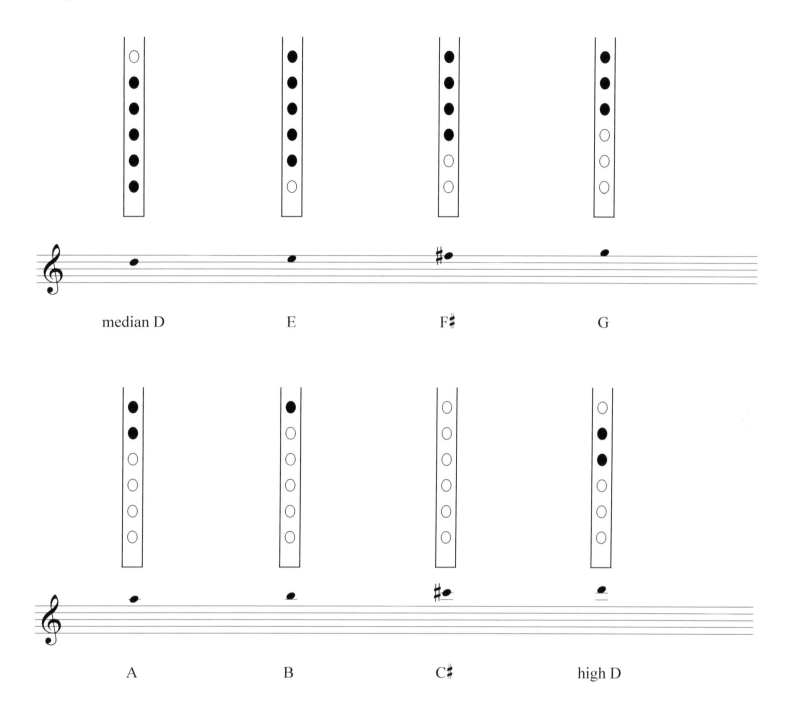

I would like to stress here that the high D note is as much about volume of breath as it is fingering, as the same fingering at a lower volume of breath brings you another (and very important) note altogether.

Before we go any farther, let me show you a drill that will increase your understanding and skill in this immensely, and right away. I call it the **Octave Drill**, and it immediately develops the body's natural ability to intuit the correct amount of breath for the note in the octave you want.

Cover all holes for the low D, and blowing a gentle low D note, suddenly increase your volume (blow harder) and at the same time, pop up your left hand index finger (see fingering chart). Then suddenly reverse the step, closing the top hole and lowering the air speed, all in one continuous breath. This should bring you from the lowest D, up to the median D, and back down again. On the musical staff, it would look like this:

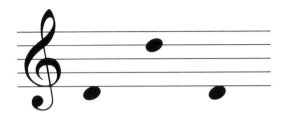

Now, cover all the holes but the lowest, and use the same breath technique for going from low E to high E and back. Repeat the pattern through all the notes: F sharp to the high F sharp and back, G to the high G and back, up to the top of the octave.

Then, beginning with the median D, go from it to the highest D and back again in one breath. Repeat with the C sharp, back down to the lowest D.

You'll see how quickly you become adept at this with just a little dedicated effort. So there you have the full two octave range of the D whistle in its natural key, D major.

But remember, earlier I mentioned that the D whistle could play in two keys, D major and G major. The key of G is attained by using a technique called cross-fingering. It flattens the C sharp down to the tone of C natural, giving you the key of G major. This is signified on the musical staff by the single sharp symbol (♯), while the key of D is represented by two sharp symbols (♯♯).

Let me describe in detail the fingerings for the G major scale. We'll begin with the low G note, which we already know. Covering only the top three holes with the left hand and blowing with the lower volume of breath, make the low G note again.

14

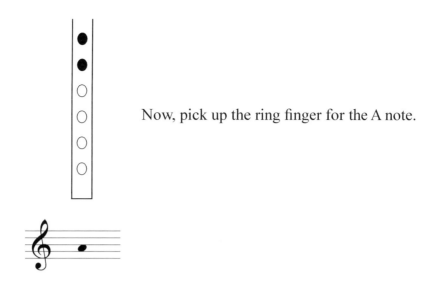

Now, pick up the ring finger for the A note.

Then, pick up the middle finger for the B note, the same as for the D scale.

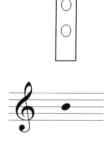

Understanding C Natural

Here, things change. We know that with all holes open, our air stream escapes mostly out the small top hole, allowing our whistle to cut the tone at C sharp. But if we cross the air stream with our fingers, going over this hole (leaving it open) but covering the two holes below it, we dampen down the air's escape out the top part of the whistle. This flattens the tone from a C sharp to a C natural.

Note now that this is the very same fingering as for the highest D note, only for this note, we use the lower volume of breath that is required for the lower octave.

Experiment! Play the C sharp with the lower volume of breath. Keep all holes open and while blowing a continuous tone, bring your fingers slowly down over the second and third holes and slowly back up again. Hear the air stream bend down to the flatter C natural? A little practice will gain you a thorough understanding of this.

The next tone up in the G major scale is the median D, fingered as before in the D scale chart. The next is the E, then the F sharp, and the octave G note. The G major fingering chart looks like this:

15

G Scale

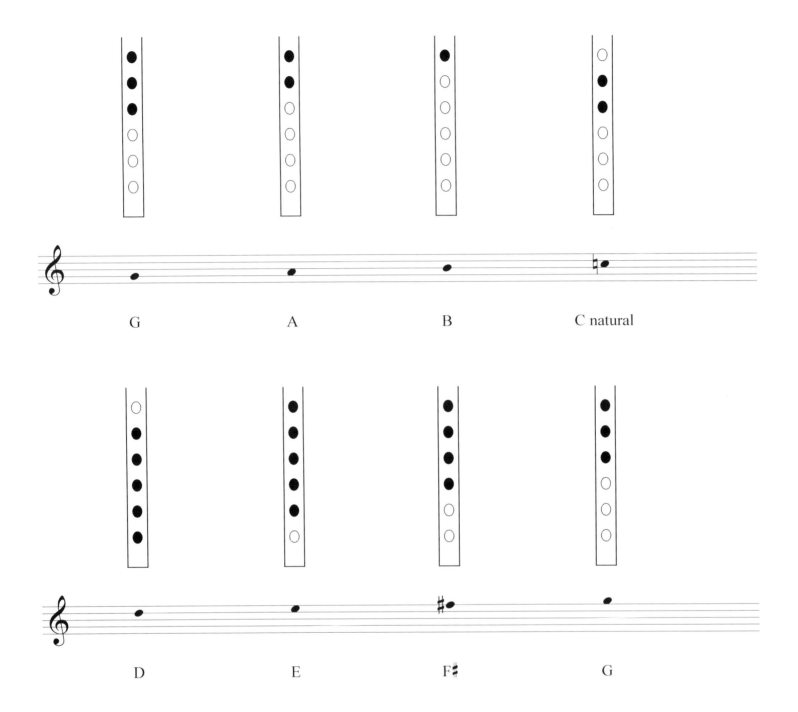

You will recognize here the familiar sounds, the familiar *sequence* of do, re, mi, fa, sol, la, ti and the octave do. This is the sequential orientation of the major scale, the same as you have with both of the octaves of D. What you are learning here is called Sol-Fa, the fundamentals of tone-scale memorization. The familiar sound of these tones *in this sequence* becomes something of a standard, which we use as a tool in learning melodies. I will discuss this more later, but first, I want to describe some fingering drills that will enable you to play this scale up and down with ease.

In one, smooth, comfortable breath, going *slowly* and with a *consciously relaxed hand,* go from:

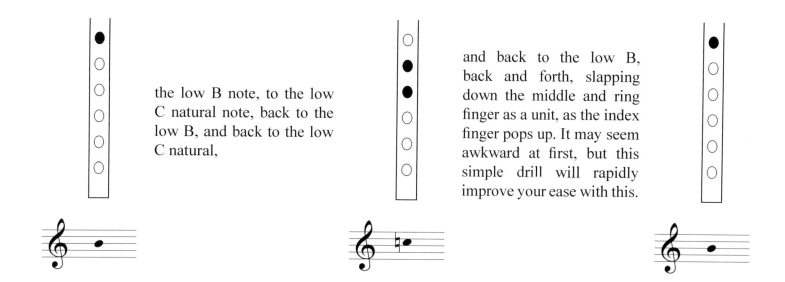

the low B note, to the low C natural note, back to the low B, and back to the low C natural,

and back to the low B, back and forth, slapping down the middle and ring finger as a unit, as the index finger pops up. It may seem awkward at first, but this simple drill will rapidly improve your ease with this.

Notes:

Now, add to the drill. Go up to the middle D by closing all the lower holes with the three fingers of the right hand while playing the low C natural. Then, pop up the fingers of the right hand to return to the C natural. Next, lift the ring and middle fingers of the left hand and put down the index finger for the B note, which on a fingering chart looks like this:

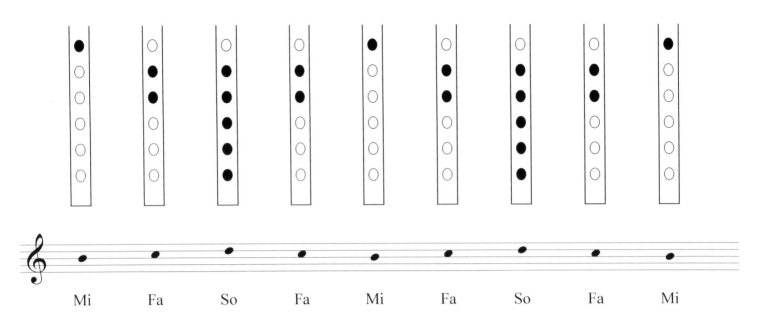

If you think this is awkward you should see what the concert flute asks of you. Don't worry. I assure you that with a little dedicated practice, this scale will come to you as easily and automatically as the D scales.

But we're not quite done! The high C sharp can be flattened down to C natural as well with a similar cross-fingering. For this note, due to the increased air speed for the highest tones, cover not only the second and third holes down leaving the top hole open, but also the fourth and fifth holes with the index and middle fingers of the right hand. Leave the bottom hole open. Use the dampering experiment, slowly covering and uncovering the second, third, fourth and fifth holes while blowing the high C sharp to get the feel for it.

Use the same drill as for the lower octave, going from the high B to high C natural and back again, to get used to it.

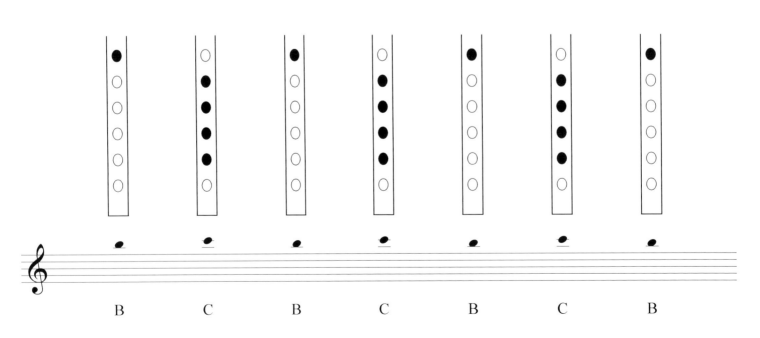

Now go from the high B up to the high D and back again.

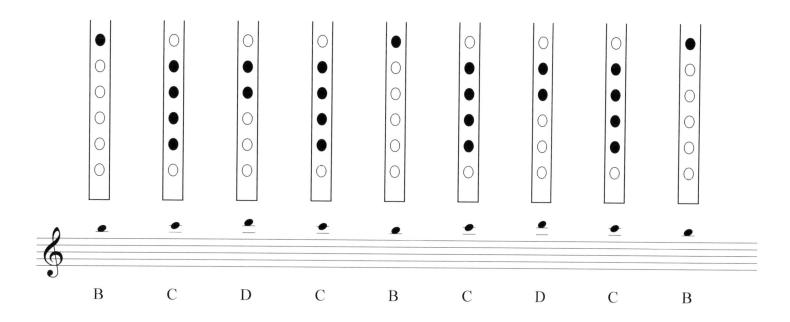

What is going on here is employment of the technique known as "putting it in your fingers." You go in one long, continuous breath from note to note and back again, slowly, and with *consciously relaxed hands*. We'll talk more about this technique later on in a more appropriate place. But for now, let me show you the exercises that will gain you fluid control over all the notes of the whistle in both the D and G key fingering patterns. What I am going to introduce to you here is a bit of classical training: the practice of scales.

Practicing Scales

Why practice scales? As you will see, playing through the scales takes you through the full range of the instrument: every note. Through repetition, finger movement becomes smooth and controlled. The airspeed becomes an automatic reflex. And breathing skills begin to build.

I want to emphasize that the practice of scales as exercises defines the difference between the aggressive, rapidly improving student and the floundering beginner. Whether or not you practice your scales will determine whether you improve quickly and comprehensively or slowly and awkwardly.

While a high school student, I had the amazing serendipity to have as my music teacher a man named Ralph Gochnour. He not only taught high school music, but played as well the position of second flute in the Utah Symphony. A graduate of the Juilliard School of Music, this talented flautist and performer could peel off the scale of every key in the chromatic system, major or minor, arpeggios and intervals, etc. It would sound just as musical as song.

Of course, I wanted to be able to play like that. Ralph's wisdom was that all musicians who take their desire to play well *seriously* spend a dedicated amount of time practicing scales. Let me reiterate: these drills are the deciding factor in whether you are going to improve quickly or slowly. A little time invested in this will bring a huge return.

About the Modes

First, I'll explain the scales we use, the Modal scales, and talk about some beneficial ways to practice them. Then, I want to say a few words about practice in general as we begin to discuss the music. It is quite simple with the whistle. We have only our six simple holes, not the collection of keys and levers so many instruments have. Nor are we concerned with a lot of key signatures and their different fingering patterns. We have only the two patterns: the key of D and the key of G.

It was in the time of the Italian predominance of the musical scene of Europe (early 1700s), that our modern system of notation was in its final evolutionary stages. As well, there was a shift in melodic structure to what we now call the use of major-minor tonality. Modern compositions, regardless of key (which then determines the pitch of the melody – high or low), tend to be one tonality or the other.

Before this development, the scales in use were called the Church Modes. There was a mode for every step of the scale and a lot of our Irish melodies were built around these more ancient tonal structures. As Miles Krassen says in his introduction to ***O'Neill's Music of Ireland, New and Revised (p.10) (1976)***:

> …[I]t should be remarked that the question of key signatures in traditional Irish music remains problematical, because the tunes in so many cases simply do not use the standard Western classical scales – and the traditional musicians of Ireland have themselves remained largely uninterested in any form of systematic theoretical analysis. The conventional major and minor scale key signatures simply do not fit the older Irish tunes, which are generally based on modal scales.

Ernest Walker, in his book *A History of Music in England*, states:

> But, after every allowance has been made, there still survives a very large and quite indubitable mass of modal music that has entirely outlasted the fashions of modern composition; and in consequence, folk tunes are, so far as tonality is concerned, the most varied of all.[1]

As a lot of our repertoire uses these old church modes, giving the melodies their different tonal characteristics, the practice of the modal scales as drills also builds a stronger familiarity with the different tonal patterns, which greatly aids in the memorization of these old tunes.

The Modes of D

We will begin with the modes of D. The first modal scale, called the Ionian, is synonymous with what we now call the major scale. The tones follow the familiar sequence of:

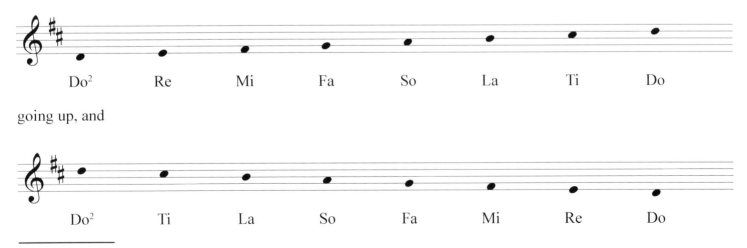

going up, and

---
[1] Walker, Ernest; *A History of Music in England*, p. 315 (1907).
[2] In medieval times, do was called "ut."

going back down again.

Take a good, comfortable lungful of air and play the scale up. Stop. Start on the median D and go back down. Now play up to the median D and back down again.

Now, you probably ran out of breath somewhere in there, going up, down, or both. I am going to talk about breathing in detail later on, but for now, simply stop, refill, and start where you left off as you need. Breathing skills will develop soon, but for now, the focus should be on covering your holes well, making whole, even sounding tones, and slow, smooth, *relaxed* finger movement between notes.

The next mode is called the Dorian. It is used very frequently in our music.

It simply begins with E instead of D, and ends on the E note one octave above. This mode has a distinctly minor sound to it, doesn't it?

The next mode, called the Phrygian, follows the same pattern, beginning on the next tone up, F sharp, and going up an octave:

The next mode, called the Lydian, goes from G to G. This sounds a lot like the major scale (the Ionian mode), but it is not. This D pattern still has a C sharp:

The next mode, the Mixolydian, begins with A for the octave:

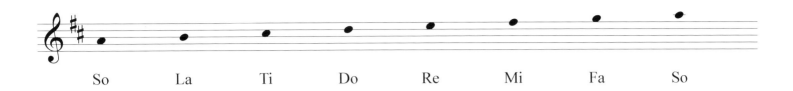

This mode sounds even more distinctly "major" than the Lydian, but for the flattened seventh, the whole tone step at the top of the scale. This mode, along with the Ionian, Dorian, and Aeolian modes, are the most frequently used in the old Irish dance tunes.

This next mode, the Aeolian, beginning with B and rising to upper B, is synonymous with the 'minor key' scale here; B being the 'relative minor' of the key of D major.

The seventh, strange sounding mode is called the Locrian, and rises from the C sharp to the high C sharp.

And the next step brings us back to the Ionian mode, one octave up. The fingering for this mode is, of course, synonymous with the chart for the high D octave, and you'll easily recognize the familiar 'major key' sequence as it begins with Do.

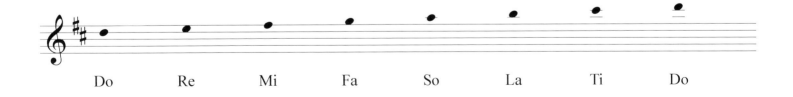

So, written out all in a row, the modes of D look and sound like this:

The Modes of G

As important to the traditional musician are the modes of G; you'll notice fully half of the tunes as written in collections, and as played in sessions, are in the key of G. There is a benefit to playing in the key of G on the D whistle in that the G series puts the range of the frequently used modes in a more central position in the whistle's two octave range, thereby giving melodies more range above and below the octave of the scale.

Also, the C natural to C sharp fingering allows us one of the few 'accidentals' (notes in a melody out of typical modal sequence) the whistle has, and the use of this as such is commonplace in the melodies. Traditional pipers call the use of this change in pitch "inflection".

Now, I am not trying to teach you a bunch of music theory here, nor is understanding music theory important to this course; but don't be intimidated by it; through application (playing music), you'll slowly gain a working knowledge of all that is really relevant to what we traditional musicians do.

To practice the modes with the key of G fingering, rather than starting with G at the bottom of the Ionian mode (the familiar sounding 'major' scale), I have found it more practical to start instead on the whistle's lowest note, the low D, which the key of G fingering starts us out with the Mixolydian mode – the same as the D scale, only remember to flat the C sharp down to C natural.

As well, you can see the diagram of the fingerings for this mode for clarity's sake.

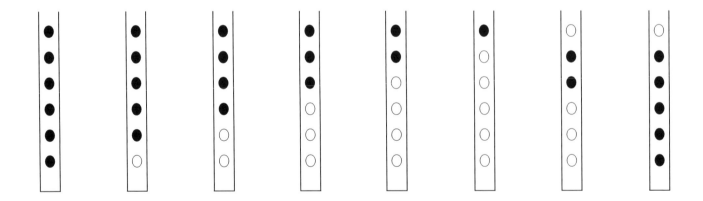

The next mode in this sequence then, is the Aeolian; the minor of the key of G. Recognize that familiar pattern? Aeolian mode:

The next step up, the Locrian mode, goes from F sharp to the upper F sharp, Locrian mode:

And the next is the Ionian mode, the key of G major. Ionian mode:

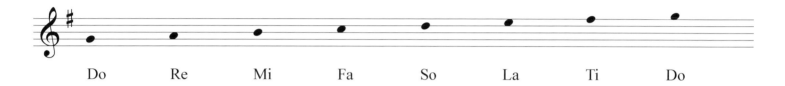

In sheet music, the single 'sharp' symbol on the F staff line means only the F is sharped (which is built in with the D whistle); the absence of the symbol on the C staff line means it is to be played 'natural,' that is, on the D whistle, flattened down from the built-in C sharp.

The Dorian mode pattern begins with A, up to high A.

The Phrygian mode begins with B, up to high B:

The Lydian mode begins with C natural, goes up to high C natural.

And then back to the Mixolydian mode again on the octave of D.

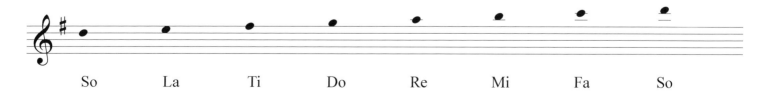

Let me diagram the fingerings for this mode once again, to allay confusion between the octaves:

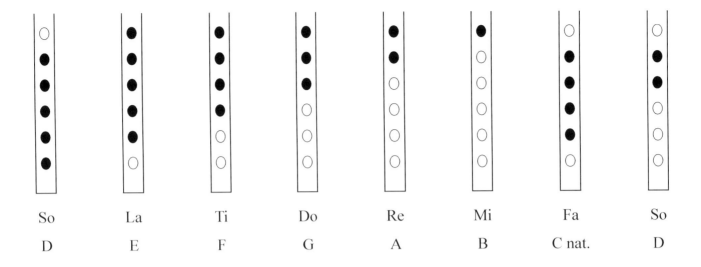

Just remember the fingerings for the highest two notes are different than for the same notes in the lower octave. A little dedicated practice and your fingers will roll right through these.

G Modes Chart

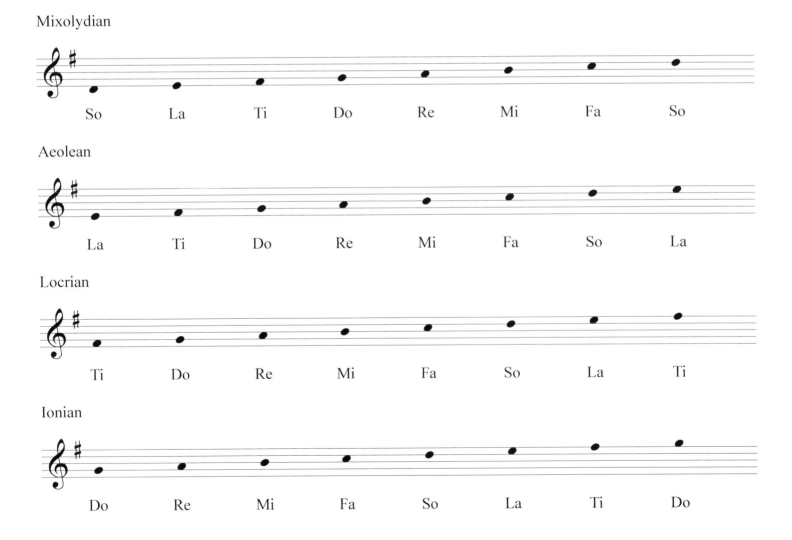

Shrill Notes and Sensitive Ears

I know these highest notes are not easy. As a matter of fact, they can be quite tough. They're loud. They're shrill. You might worry about breaking nearby windows. We have this in common with students of the trumpet, saxophone, drum-kit, and bagpipes (to name a few): we're loud. You will gain control over these high, piercing tones only by playing them repetitively, but when you're first learning, they're often so shrill you tend to 'back away' a bit and not give the tones the power they need. So wear earplugs, like the bagpipers do. The little foam things you get at the hardware store work fine. This will take the edge off the shrillness so you won't shy away from the high notes in practice.

I want to outline some very beneficial ways to use these scales in your practice time next, and talk specifically about practice as we begin to discuss learning the music.

Practice

It might, from what I've written so far, seem as though I expect the beginner to just hammer away at scales and drills, but this is not the case. Of course, you will have to practice – that is, if you want to get any good at it, and you won't practice if you don't enjoy it. So there's a strategy to develop then, to make practice enjoyable and recreational, and it includes the practice of these scales. You see, in giving the whistle a try, you will be giving over some time to it; and this time you spend can be used effectively or ineffectively. If your practice time is unstructured, without a plan and firm direction, your attention is likely to wander, your progress will be slow and inconsistent, and you may lose interest. But if you're improving rapidly for the time you put in – gaining noticeably in ability for every hour you put into it – that can be pretty motivating! And you must see results to enjoy the learning or you will eventually lose interest. Let me relate my experience as there might be something to learn from it.

"A crucial factor in successful, ongoing learning is *routine*."[3]

I'm an apartment dweller in the Big City; and my roommates and neighbors could not work with my desire to practice a little before leaving for my job at 6:30 a.m., so I would simply leave home an hour early and stop off at a park, or go to my favorite place, a huge parking lot next to a stadium in the industrial part of town. This had a freeway viaduct not very far away, creating a convenient backdrop of white noise. A band of Highland pipers could have drilled there and bothered no one. So I had a sense of privacy, which I feel is important. As jazzman Charlie Parker once said, "You went out to the woodshed where you could be alone and wouldn't freak your folks, and you made all the mistakes you needed, because that's how you would learn."[4] If you can't find a place or a time at home where you won't be bothering someone, maybe use the quieter conical Clark whistle, or switch to the lower, mellower C whistle. I chose to practice in the morning for the same reason most runners pick the morning, when you have all your energy before a hard day's work. This soon became a cherished routine: a valuable time to myself, apart from the day's usual intrusions.

Remembering Ralph's phrase, "If you want to improve, you'll practice the scales," or something to that effect, and knowing I wasn't going to "get them down" anytime soon, even if that's all I did, I proposed to myself to plan to practice scales and drills just a little disciplined while each day; if not half my time, then at least 10-15 minutes. I would practice the modes of D one day and the modes of G the next. I would note the time on my watch and for 10 minutes or so, concentrate on going through the various scales, *slowly and with deliberately relaxed hands*, focusing on covering my holes completely (making whole sounding tones), and making the exchanges between notes clean and evenly timed, like Ralph had taught me to do on a concert flute. Now, the octave drill, the high note drills, and what follows are part of what I was referring to early on when I mentioned a program for rapid improvement, so let me go into detail here.

I would start with the low D note, and using either the D pattern or the G pattern, would play up to the top of the mode, stop, and beginning with the highest note of the mode, go back down again. I would repeat this one mode four times, then progress to the next mode in the scale and go up, then down it four times, and so on up through all the modes four times, then the highest another four, and repeat the same pattern down again. Even this alone would take up to ten minutes; then, I would spend a few minutes with the high note drills and the octave drill. The rest of my time, I would prod away at learning tunes.

---

[3] Lewis, Norman, ***Word Power Made Easy***.
[4] Carson, Ciaran. ***Last Night's Fun***, p. 52.

The Learning Curve

I want to say something about the learning curve here, and I think it's important to be aware of this. Teaching your fingers to make carefully timed, delicate movements isn't easily done. It takes some dedication, especially at first, when a pattern that seems like it should be so straightforward proves to be (at first) so awkward and frustrating. A feature of the learning curve here is that it often starts with a dip; what I mean is, after the first day of trying to learn smooth, controlled finger movement, you might find it more awkward the second day, and even worse the next. It might be that it takes a certain amount of time for the conscious mind to relinquish control to the subconscious reflex. Be patient here; keep persisting, even though 10 to 15 minutes a day on loud drills you seem to be getting worse at is pretty hard to take. You'll notice in your first week of consistent practice a sudden turn around. You'll begin practice and at once feel like you're 'getting it' – your fingers will be moving more evenly, with more control. Your breath will begin to work in closer synch. This is because not only your mind, but your body has to learn this new form of language and your sub-conscious mind, which is the connecting rod, needs time to catch up to the task that your conscious, deliberate practice has set up for it to absorb. You could think of it as teaching your fingers and breath to dance together. When I first felt my fingers begin to develop that ease of movement, I knew I'd eventually get it!

A Most Beneficial Drill

Another drill with the modes is playing them four times each as described, but go up the scale and back down again in one breath. If you can't quite yet, here's another way to practice the modes that does more to develop breathing skills. Play up the scale to an even beat, taking a breath on time instead of the octave note, which for the D Ionian mode would sound like this:

Do	Re	Mi	Fa	So	La	Ti	(breath)	Do	Ti	La	So	Fa	Mi	Re	Do
1	2	3	4	5	6	7	and	1	2	3	4	5	6	7	8

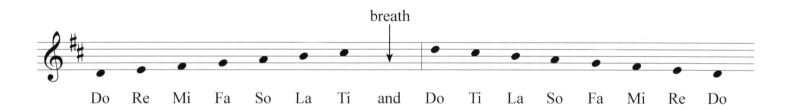

Try playing this pattern up and down each mode of both scale patterns, D and G. Go from one repetition to the next, keeping the beat, breathing only at the top, and tapping out the beat with your foot. You'll rapidly see how intimately connected rhythm and breathing are. You can't keep rhythm until you learn how to breathe, *and you won't learn to breathe until you can keep rhythm!* I show how to overcome this paradox when we discuss rhythm and tempo later on.

So, I've explained the whistle and its range, how to play the notes, and some ways to build skill and control. Now let's talk about the music; how to learn it and how to play it.

The Music

If you've been to a traditional session at an Irish pub, you've no doubt seen players peel off tune after tune after tune, and all from memory, with only the barest of cues to jump from one to the next. Sure, talent helps, but this is a learned skill; one that anyone with some musical inclination and the sincere desire can pick up. Playing from memory is the standard among traditional musicians. That is why the focus of this book is about learning and playing by ear, not learning to sight read sheet music. Remember – if you want to play from the heart, you must learn by heart.

Let's begin our discussion with a few relevant quotes:

> Few musicians have been found to question the assertion that Irish folk-music is, on the whole, the finest that exists; it ranges with wonderful ease over the whole gamut of human emotion from the cradle to the battlefield, and is unsurpassed in poetical and artistic charm. If musical composition meant nothing more than tunes sixteen bars long, Ireland could claim some of the very greatest composers that have ever lived; for in their miniature form, the best Irish folk tunes are gems of absolutely flawless luster, and though of course some of them are relatively undistinctive, it is very rare to meet with one entirely lacking in character.[5]

and

> …[W]hen at their best, they give us melody that the greatest composers would have been proud to sign.[6]

There's something very key to learning these melodies referred to in this. This next quote comes from the introduction to ***O'Neill's Dance Music of Ireland***, published in 1907, and refers to the publication of his (O'Neill's) first collection, ***O'Neill's Music of Ireland***, which was published four years before:

> For over a third of a century I have been waiting, watching, hoping and praying, that God might inspire some Irishman, or association of Irishmen, to collect and publish just such a work as "The Music of Ireland" – the grand old music – the weird, beautiful, wild and mournful reel tunes that entranced me when a child, a youth, and a man, in the street or barn, at the bonfire or on the hilltop; the music, the never-to-be-forgotten strains that often made my blood alternately flame or freeze- that made me when a child, sitting beneath the fiddler's chair, weep with delight or sadness, a condition of mind impossible to describe. Many of the grand old tunes learned from the lips of my poor dead mother, which I had not heard since childhood, and still others that I had heard played when a boy, were floating about in my memory, disconnected, and fragmentary, before your book came. Well, dear sir, I thank God that I have lived to see my dreams realized, and my prayer answered more fully than my wildest ambition had dared to go.[7]

In this as well we see a key to memorization.

Let's first talk about memory in a general way; then we'll get down to the particulars that make the jigs, reels, and other dance tunes that comprise the session repertoire particularly easy to learn and remember.

Almost everything our mind keeps available to us in our memory is there because of either repetition or association. There are other means that will deftly imprint things upon one's memory – the shock of a sudden surprise for instance. But by and large, most of the things we retain in the well of our memory, particularly those things close to the surface, are present there because we've seen, heard, or otherwise experienced them over and over again, or because they remind us of something, that is, are easily associated with something that we're already familiar with due to repetitive exposure. Advertising in the modern communications media makes use of this with diabolical mastery, assaulting the sensibilities as repetitively as possible, using imagery, both visual and

---

[5] Walker, Ernest; *A History of Music in England*, p. 334.
[6] *Id.* p. 313.
[7] Patrick O'Leary of Adelaide, So. Australia.

aural (melodies, sound effects) to conjure any relevant associations already in your mind that will cause you to remember their product, sale, store or what have you (*e.g.*: the advertising jingle you really wish you could forget, or the use of Beethoven's "Ode to Joy" to promote a laundry detergent).

There's another aspect of memory. Sure, we're prone to remember what we see and hear and otherwise experience repetitively, or to be able to recall that which is easily associated with something already solidly familiar, but you'll notice the things that are most easily remembered are the things that have had *an emotional impact*, that is, the things that remind you somehow of something that had an effect on your feelings, and the deeper the imprint on your feelings, the more easily is the memory recalled to the conscious mind. The quote from Patrick O'Leary makes it clear that many of the melodies we are discussing, though, "floating about in my memory, disconnected and fragmentary" were there at all because they were the "never to be forgotten strains that often made my blood alternately flame or freeze, that made me…weep with delight or sadness, a condition of mind impossible to describe."

Impressions on the Memory

Let's hear what Francis O'Neill, the celebrated collector, had to say on the subject:

> Music it must be granted surpasses every other aid to memory in that it brings its influence most directly and most movingly to the heart. The old song or strain possesses a power which will turn back the years even to the cradle no less than the odor of forgotten flowers. We must not forget, however, that memory is capricious, and preserves a baffling independence of the will. We cannot always summon up forthwith the images or combination of tones which we desire. Neither can the untrained ear be always relied on when we wish to reproduce the words or musical forms casually impressed on it.[8]

Music, the indefinitive language of the emotions, is often imprinted in our memory as a component, and a vital one, of a specific experience. I want to speak briefly about some childhood experiences of mine, and then about Francis O'Neill's.

My mother is a lover of classical music and as a child, I was exposed to the repetitive playing of the classical greats on the radio, with which my mother would sing along, 'lilting' the essential melodies from the symphonic music of Brahms, Beethoven, Mozart and the rest. Over the years, I heard these many times, and with the instinctively inquisitive mind of a child, I took in stimulus and made associations along with these melodies in abundance. So then, in the same years that I learned to speak and identify ideas as words, I learned melodies, and the various patterns and types of melodies, and how to differentiate between them, how to analyze and catalogue them, and how to recall them as well as, and in somewhat the same way as, the language of words.

According to Gearóid Ó hAllmhuráin, in the introduction to his book, *A Pocket History of Irish Traditional Music*: "Experienced musicians are capable of memorizing up to 500 pieces of music, some of which they play regularly, while others may lie dormant for years."[9]

Frank O'Neill was undoubtedly in this league, as evinced by the stories told in the memoirs regarding his experiences as a collector. Let's see what historians have to say of O'Neill's childhood:

> Francis O'Neill, christened Daniel and familiarly known as Frank, was born in Tralibane[10] on 28 August 1848, the youngest of seven children. Although he was born during the Great Famine, the ravages of which were becoming less severe at the time of his birth, O'Neill would have had no personal memories of it. His native parish of Caheragh in the Union of Skibbereen, part of an

---

[8] O'Neill, Francis. *Irish Minstrels and Musicians*, (1913). p. 126.
[9] *Pocket History of Irish Traditional Music*, The O'Brien Press, (1998), p. 6.
[10] Tralibane is three miles S.E. of the coastal town of Bantry, Co. Cork.

intensively potato-growing region, was catastrophically affected by the potato blight. Corpses of those who had died from hunger and fever floated down the Ilen, and Skibbereen became a byword for famine throughout Ireland and beyond. The starving children at Caheragh in James Mahoney's famous 1847 sketches for *The Illustrated London News* were O'Neill's contemporaries, and he may have known them, if they survived. O'Neill, however, makes no personal allusion to the Famine in his voluminous writings, and only occasional passing references to its effects on music in the country in general. Bantry and its hinterland seem to have recovered quickly from the worst effects of the Famine, and O'Neill's formative years were spent in a period in which agricultural activity increased and the area began to open up to tourism and trade.

…

Music, song and dance were an integral part of the largely Irish speaking rural society in which O'Neill grew up, and his father's house and that of a sister were venues for neighborhood dances. Pipers, fiddle players and flute players were frequently heard at crossroad dances in summer and at farmhouse dances in winter. The parish supported two professional Pipers in the years after the Famine: Charley Murphy, or 'Cormac na bPaidreacha', who had a regular outdoor pitch at Tralibane Bridge, a few hundred yards from the O'Neill home, and Peter Hagerty, 'An Piobaire Bán', who played at the nearby Colomane crossroads. The latter made an indelible impression on the young O'Neill:

"With what wonder and curiosity we youngsters gazed on this musical wizard, as he disjointed his drones and regulators and tested the reeds and quills with his lips…Being young and insignificant I was put to bed, out of the way, while the others went to enjoy the dance next door. It just chanced that the piper was seated close to the partition wall…Half asleep and awake the music hummed in my ears for hours, and the memory of the tunes is still vivid after the lapse of fifty years."

…

O'Neill's teacher owned a large collection of music in manuscript, but he does not seem to have taught his pupil to read music, a skill that O'Neill acquired to some degree years later in America.[11]

Here is Frank, himself:

The rudiments of music on the flute were kindly taught me by Mr. Timothy Downing, a gentleman farmer in Tralibane, our townland. He was an accomplished performer on several instruments, but the violin was his favorite. He never played outside his own residence, and there only for a favored few. Humming a tune as he played it, was one of his peculiarities.[12]

Let's examine one once popular American melody, and why in particular it's so memorable.

Andy of Mayberry

As a child growing up in the early 1960's, as well as my mom and her wonderful radio, there was a T.V. set (in these days, television was only becoming ubiquitous, and the broadcasting shut down at night to the national anthem). There was a show, very popular with just about everyone, called the Andy Griffith show. This T.V. show had a particular theme tune (interestingly, in two parts of eight bars each) which was whistled with the lips in a jaunty, nonchalant way, to the rhythmic snap of fingers.

---

[11] Carolan, Nicholas, *A Harvest Saved: Francis O'Neill and Irish Music in Chicago*, (1997). p. 5-7.
[12] O'Neill, Francis, *Irish Folk Music – A Fascinating Hobby*, (1910). p. 15.

Besides the melody, there was the video image to associate with it – a warm, friendly, pleasantly bucolic scene. I might not remember the visual image with great accuracy – I think it was the popular sheriff of the small town featured in the show with his son, walking a country road – but I remember the theme tune note for note, and I'm sure I'm not the only one. Now, why is that?

Well, one aspect here is repetition; that show ran for years and years; I and those of my generation must have seen it and heard that theme literally hundreds of times. And another aspect is association. Having a visual image intimately connected with it; an image of warm happiness, easily sentimentalized and personalized.

An image that provokes an emotional response is a powerful tool in conjuring a melody from the memory to the conscious mind, just as a melody can trigger the memory of an image or event.

Think of how we remember, for instance, the name of someone new to you. If, upon introduction, it's a name I've never heard before, I'll often have a difficult time remembering it at first. But if it's a name that I already am acquainted with, say Julie, upon meeting this new Julie I'll picture – I'll imagine – this new Julie alongside a Julie I already know, with their arms over each other's shoulder as if they were good friends of the same name posing for a picture while having a good time together. The stronger the emotional charge to the association, and the more detailed the imagery associated, the better the ability to recall the name of the new person. It is in these ways the mind, both consciously and subconsciously, develops the tools of deliberate memory retention.

So What's in a Name?

You've heard the frivolous expression, "What's in a name?" – an image, most often a memory of some kind. Names themselves are a mnemonic device. Names can trigger the recollection of complex systems of huge dimension, as in Biology, Mathematics or Physics. Words, in general, are for the most part simply the nomenclature of ideas. So a name can easily provoke the recollection of an image, or a collection of images and impressions, as well as, with practice, the recollection of a melody, though the subconscious associations that occur to cause a melody to rise from the memory at the mention of a name may themselves not become obvious. But regardless, the tune surfaces in the conscious mind at the mention of the name only if *somehow an emotional bond has been created between the two*, through imagery and associated memories.

You'll probably discover someday upon learning a tune with an unknown name, that you'll give it some sort of name yourself; after all, the names of the tunes are 99% of the time monikers only, and have no other connection whatsoever with the melody. Often, tunes are known by more than one name, which helps explain why sometimes the names may not seem quite suited to the emotional character of the tune all that well. Some tunes, having no name or an unfamiliar word for a name, will try to slip away into the past, while others carry perhaps a few too many monikers. For instance, "Rolling in the Rye Grass," according to Breandan Breathnach's "Ceol Rince na hEireann", is known also as

Maureen Playboy,
Old Molly Aterhn,
The Piper's Lass,
The Rathkeale Hunt,
The Shannon Breeze,
The Lady's Top Dress,
The Lady's Tight Dress
The Telegraph
What the Devil Ails Him
Roll Her on the Banks
The Railway Station
The Connachtman's Ramble

> McCaffrey's Reel,
> What the Devil Ails You?
> The Lady on the Railroad
> The Brown Red Girl,
> Love Among the Roses,
> The Kilfinane Reel
> The Listowel Lasse
> Boil the Kettle Early,
> Kitty Got a Clinking (also the name of a completely different reel); and
> Punch for the Ladies[13]

Of course, the focus being on remembering the melody, one name is adequate, as long as it helps recall the melody.

Whatever it is, as long as the name helps conjure the sound of the melody it applies to, that is the required result. So you see, though a tune's name is really of little importance beyond nomenclature, it can be a valuable tool for remembering a melody if the melody, the name of the melody, and an emotionally charged image associated with both are packaged in to the memory as a unit. And remember: the greater the imprint on the emotions, the stronger the grasp by the memory.

Well, so far I've argued the point that exposure to music as a child has a huge value in cultivating the ability to memorize melody; also intimated the point that a vivid imagination plays a large role. I mentioned television earlier, which I would like to say decreases, actually does damage, to your child's ability to form mental imagery by doing much too much of the imaging for the child's mind. On the other hand, reading, in particular books – fiction or non-fiction – with a substantial story line and deep character development, force the imagination to form its own imagery, thereby increasing and strengthening not only the mind's ability to create images, but also the mind's ability to recall the specific imagery it seeks from the memory.

Now, I would like to draw the focus down to the specifics on how to memorize the Irish session repertoire, the "weird, beautiful, wild and mournful" reels, jigs, slip-jigs, and hornpipes of Scotland and Ireland.

Immersion

Just like learning a new language by moving to a country where little else is spoken, if you can, immerse yourself in the old tunes, that is, at least for awhile, try and listen to little else. Let's return once again to the Irish childhood of Frank O'Neill.

> Being a music lover rather than a musician, no jealousies or
> rivalries ever marred our friendly relations.
> In course of time I became aware of the fact that I was the
> custodian of a great many airs and dance tunes, unconsciously
> memorized in my boyhood days, not known to any of them.[14]

---

[13] Carson, Ciaran, **Last Night's Fun**, (1996). p. 8.

[14] Chief O'Neill, **Sketchy Recollections of an Eventful Life in Chicago**, (2008), p. 166-67.

Mid-nineteenth century Ireland was what we now think of as a simpler time – I'm sure life in post-famine Ireland had its own complexities, but it was entirely free of the aforementioned television, the radio, the computer, e-mails, Blackberries, video games, VCRs, CDs, DVDs, the seemingly ubiquitous iPods, flip-phones, laptops, etc., etc., *ad nauseum*, that crowd our waking hours, harry our nerves, and continually stuff our conscious minds way beyond capacity with largely meaningless, unimportant piles of data that dwarf even a sentence like this one.

Like I say, I'm sure they were busy with other things in the old days – but their *minds* had more time – less constant stimulation from all quarters, more time to reflect, to think, to *process*. Students of meditation are well aware of the value of this.

Frank O'Neill had the serendipity to grow up immersed in this beautiful music, and just like a language, its *forms and structures* became second nature to him. So what I'm telling you here is not to try to have an Irish childhood, but to try as best you can to immerse yourself in the music – to the exclusion of all other entertainments for awhile, and to *give your mind some quiet time*. Your mind needs both time and room to absorb this new musical idiom. I know it's tough to ask of a modern person, but if you can listen to nothing but the jigs and reels for an extended amount of time, other music or entertainment as little as possible for the longer the better, you will be giving yourself an immeasurable step forward in developing your musical ability, simply by listening, and by giving your mind some time to think over and process what you've taken in.

You'll notice right away, if you do this, that as you work your way through your daily grind, the tunes you've been listening to, and typically your favorite ones, will start surfacing in the back of your mind as your subconscious mind works through its myriad of daily puzzles. The constant, mathematical form and symmetrically inclined melodic structures are, through repetition, easily analyzed and categorized for the memory. Just like the advertising jingle you wish you could forget, if you consciously make an effort to saturate yourself with the jigs and reels, they will begin to take over as the soundtrack of your subconscious.

Let's Learn a Tune

Well now, knowing how to make tones from playing scales, let's learn a tune! This book being in part about how to memorize the tunes, I'm not going to give you some sheet music here and teach you to follow the dots and lines. Instead, what I want you to do is listen to some recordings of the dance music, the more traditional the artists' styles and the less elaborate the studio production the better (actually, a tape recording from a session would be perfect), and find a tune: a jig, reel, hornpipe, or whatever, one that you really *like* (you've probably already done this); one that you think is 'catchy,' or beautiful or unique, or very attractive to you in some way – this is the tune you want to start with. Not necessarily one that sounds simple and easy to play, but one that 'strikes a chord' with you, as this is the one you'll more easily remember, and hence more easily learn.

Just as the ancient pipe-masters, in teaching the "Pibrachs," the classical music of the bagpipe, would require their students to be able to 'lilt' (that is, sing) the often lengthy, complex melodies to them in full before they would allow them to attempt it on the pipes; we must know our melody in our mind (or as it's said, 'by heart') before we attempt to play it on the whistle. Music occurs first in the imagination.

You've accomplished the first step if you've found a tune that, for whatever reason, you find emotionally compelling, and the more so the better.

And now, we apply repetition. Listen to a recording of the tune one hundred times, and I mean this, literally one hundred times. Listen to the cassette tape or CD track it's on, back it up, listen again, back it up, listen again, on and on and over and over; I found being stuck in rush hour traffic a great opportunity for this. Here, we have the modern technology working for us; we have a way to repeat the tune back at our whim. Think back to the simpler times, the aspiring musician might only hear a tune he desires to learn perhaps a few times a night in a pub, at best; but his advantage was in the fewer distractions to the mind and memory, and long familiarity with the idiom. Another advantage of the simpler times; not being able to re-wind and play it again at whim, paradoxically. Remember: the human mind is naturally inquisitive and drawn to puzzles. The memory gains strength from the knowledge that it has only its own skills to fall back on. For this reason, Frank O'Neill, in spite of being a collector of written melodies, abstained from reading sheet music until relatively late in life, as apparently he felt doing so would blunt his ability to pick up tunes as easily by ear. As he says in his book, **Irish Minstrels and Musicians**,

> "The saying that the invention of writing injured the power of memory finds much support from the fact that musicians, ignorant of written music, possess the faculty of memorizing tunes to a far greater degree than those who acquire their repertory from that source."[15]

If we listen to a tune for one hundred repetitions (over the course of a few days, of course), and then allow ourselves some quiet time where we consciously apply ourselves to recalling bits of the melody, the tune will indeed begin to surface in the conscious mind, just like the bad advertising jingle you couldn't wait to forget, but you must give your memory a chance; and that means not only some time, but have some faith in yourself. As the mind becomes practiced at this, tunes are of course acquired much more quickly, but at first just be patient. Drown yourself in the tunes you wish to learn for the one hundred repetitions. It won't always take this much time and energy, but at first, the process is slow as the subconscious mind assembles the necessary tools for the task at hand. However, once a few tunes have been learned entirely by ear, the process rapidly gains in ease.

This technique has helped musicians who can sight read fluently, but have a tough time recalling a melody once the book is closed.

Neither harpers nor pipers made use of printed music even when available in the eighteenth and nineteenth centuries, as in fact, the majority of them were blind and of necessity obliged to learn and teach by the oral method only.[16]

Analytical Listening

These fundamentals having been discussed, we can narrow down the discussion to Analytical Listening, or, how to understand the form and dissect the parts of the melody we're learning. This is where it really becomes fun, and very systematic.

I'm sure you've noticed this music is rigidly structured in pattern and very mathematical in its framework. Understanding what you are hearing is key, and learning how to categorize.

The main division between all types of melodies is in what we call Time: how many beats per measure. This can be expressed in different ways in musical notation (time signatures), but to the ear, the heart of the matter is this: there are two distinct groups of melodies – those in binary time (in multiples of two) and ternary time (in multiples of three).

---

[15] O'Neill, Francis. *Irish Minstrels and Musicians*, (1913). p. 126.
[16] *Ibid.*

What a particular melody is in time wise is easily deduced by ear with a simple formula, and this draws the distinction between what tune is of the Jig family; that is, jigs, double jigs, and slip or hop jigs, and which is of the Reel family: the reels, hornpipes, marches, polkas, and others of the dance music. And the formula helps you recall the name of the type as well, as jigs, in their ternary (counts of three) time can be counted out using the three letters

$$J-I-G, J-I-G, 1-2-3, 1-2-3, J-I-G$$

These beats are to be counted out as evenly as the ticking of a clock. An apt formula to apply to a melody is to count along with the syllables

Dye – del – dee   Dye – del – dee

Dye – del – dee   Dye – del – dee

Dye – del – dee   Dye – del – dee

Dye – del – dee   Dye – del – dee

– if this rhythmic pattern fits the melody you're analyzing, then it's either a Jig (single or double, this is a dancer's distinction only), or a hop jig. Slip, or Hop jigs are in 9/8 time, still a ternary count, but rather than two groups of three counts per 'measure':

Dye – del – dee   Dye – del – dee
1   2   3   1   2   3

Dye – del – dee   Dye – del – dee
1   2   3   1   2   3

There are three, like:

Dye – del – dee   Dye – del – dee   Dye – del – dee
1   2   3   4   5   6   7   8   9

Dye – del – dee   Dye – del – dee   Dye – del – dee
1   2   3   4   5   6   7   8   9

A similar syllabic aid works with the reel family, which tunes are written in 4/4, or what's called 'common' time, as are hornpipes, with polkas often being written in 2/4 time. This syllabic aid also works with the letters R-E-E-L. Say it evenly, like a chant:

Oogah – chucka – oogah – chucka

Oogah – chucka – oogah – chucka

Oogah – chucka – Oogah – chucka – Oogah – chucka
1 2   3 4   1 2   3 4   1 2   3 4

Oogah – chucka – Oogah – chucka – Oogah – chucka
1 2   3 4   1 2   3 4   1 2   3 4

You get the picture. So, first thing, apply these syllabic chants to the tempo of the music, and the one that works with the rhythmic cadence of the tune will tell you immediately what time group it's in.

I should explain here that the difference between reels, hornpipes, polkas, and others in the common time family, is solely one of rhythmic emphasis. Reels are typically played with a quick tempo; but much more importantly, the rhythm is smooth and even, a steady, non-fluctuating count of:

1 2 3 4 1 2 3 4 1 2 3 4 1 2 3 4 1 2 3 4

as opposed to the hornpipe, which is typically played slower and more deliberately; but again, and much more importantly, has a distinct lope to the way it's played, as in:

OO – gah – CHU – cka – OO – gah – CHU – cka
1-2   3   1-2   3   1-2   3   1-2   3

OO – gah – CHU – cka – OO – gah – CHU – cka
1-2   3   1-2   3   1-2   3   1-2   3

ONE two THREE four ONE two THREE four

ONE two THREE four ONE two THREE four

(Hornpipes were actually written in 3/2 time up until about 1760).

Sometimes, Hornpipes are written out using 'dotted' notes to help convey the 'lope' effect intended for the rhythm, but as this leads to unnecessary confusion, most authors of collections print them in simple 4/4 time, assuming the musician will know from the identifier "Hornpipe" the correct type of loping rhythm and slow tempo to give it. This rhythm has to be heard to be understood and learned, as sheet music cannot correctly convey it.[17]

Polkas have the same even count as the reel; but again, a slower, pedestrian pace with a pronounced one-two 'step' to the emphasis, as in:

OOM – pah   OOM – pah

OOM – pah   OOM – pah

or perhaps:

ONE   and   TWO   and

ONE   and   TWO   and

You'll often hear that rhythm at the Oktoberfest, or maybe the county fair.

So then, the first step in analyzing a tune is to determine what rhythmic family it's in; if it's a reel or a jig or what have you, and then, how many parts it has.

---

[17] See Appendix 2.

Parts

Whether it's a jig in 6/8 time, or a reel or hornpipe in 4/4 time, the dance tunes follow an identical, and very regimented pattern. This is the nature of this music, and an essential aspect of the traditional playing; that it follows a regimented pattern with set parameters that other musicians will understand and anticipate. The foundation of this pattern is the 'part,' a melody eight bars long, a 'bar' being a certain number of beats. Whatever the melody you're trying to learn does, it does it all within its concise little frame of eight bars, including any melodic bridges to the next part, which may be of a markedly different emotional character than the first. The tunes always have two parts; often more, but always two parts, for a total of 16 bars. Hearken back to what Ernest Walker had to say in the former quote:

> If musical composition meant nothing more than tunes 16 bars long, Ireland could claim some of the very greatest composers who have ever lived, for in their miniature form, the best Irish folk tunes are gems of absolutely flawless luster…

And these 'gems' are never more than eight bars per part. This is key: the melody will always fit in its miniature rhythmic 'box,' and then move to the next, identically sized time frame, before either repeating or returning to the former.

> "With the exception of a score or so of tunes to which special dances are performed, all these tunes share a similar structure. Each consists of at least two strains or parts of eight bars – there are no dance tunes and only very few airs, which have only one strain. In the vast majority of tunes, each part is made up of two phrases. The common pattern is a single phrase repeated with some slight modification, with the phrases falling naturally into half-phrases of two bars each. A basic element present alike in song and dance music is exhibited in these half-phrases; the first making, as it were, an assertion to which the second is the response. This principal of contrast is present to some extent even between the two phrases of a strain, although as suggested, the melodic differences, if any, may be only slight."[18]

So, what I'm saying is the melody of an eight bar part will take up this much space – if a jig, it will fit in the time frame of:

1   Dye – del – dee   Dye – del – dee

2   Dye – del – dee   Dye – del – dee

3   Dye – del – dee   Dye – del – dee

4   Dye – del – dee   Dye – del – dee

5   Dye – del – dee   Dye – del – dee

6   Dye – del – dee   Dye – del – dee

7   Dye – del – dee   Dye – del – dee

8   Dye – del – dee   Dye – del – dee

---

[18] Breathnach, Breandán. *Folk Music and Dances of Ireland*, (1996). p. 56.

On the musical graph, that is, Staff lines (the horizontal lines notes are written on) that could be drawn like this:

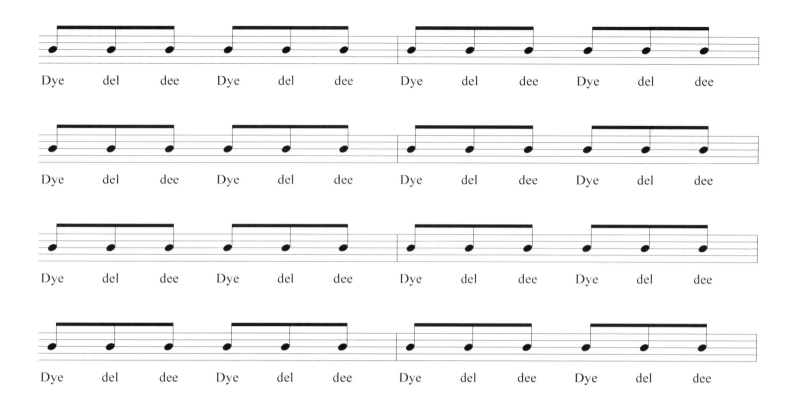

If the tune is a reel, it will fit in the time frame of:

So what you're hearing when you listen to a jig or a reel is a systematic arrangement of these 8-bar parts in this order: Part A, then A will be repeated. Then the B part is played, and it as well is repeated. If there is a third part, C, it follows, and is likewise repeated, and the same with any subsequent parts. Then the whole frame is played again at least once (as many times as you like, but at least once), creating a pattern that in performance sounds like this:

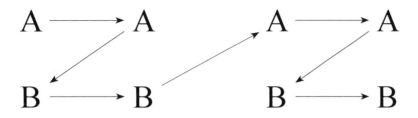

for a two part tune, or:

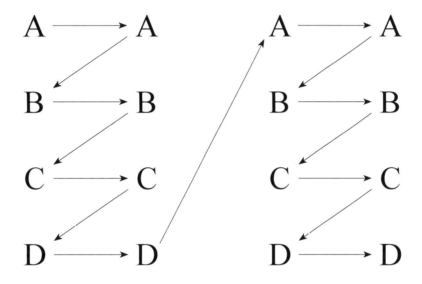

for a tune of four parts. In this way, a simple sixteen bar melody can be turned into a substantial performance of a couple of minutes' duration.

Primes

There is an exception that frequently turns up, which we call a 'prime.' A prime is a part that, rather than being eight bars of melody, which is repeated, instead has a pronounced variation as an accepted part of the tune for the repetition. Metrically, this has the effect of creating a 16-bar part. These sometimes show up in the A part of a tune (the 'tune'), but more often in the B part (the 'turn'), which brings me to mention a few words about how the music is played. Let's say a musician is playing a two part jig, hence working through the pattern:

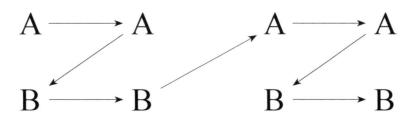

An example of a first part prime from Miles Krassen's collection:

The Reel of Mullinavat

Now, if he's good, and knows his tune and his idiom well, what he'll do is play the A part in say, the familiar, commonly known (at least to him) way but the second time through will play it just a little differently, - not only substituting different ornaments for the ones used the first time through, but even minor melodic variations: adding notes (but not time value), dropping notes, moving 'quavers' (groups of notes) around, changing the 'phrasing' by altering the rhythmic emphasis (compressing or expanding the time value of certain notes), you name it! The ability to fluently perform in this fashion is seen as the paragon of the idiom. We'll discuss this in greater depth later, but for now, the question is how do you learn a melody when each time you hear a part played through, it's played differently than the time before? What you'll find with this music is that there are often several 'settings' or variations of the same basic melody, and furthermore, individual interpretation can make them sound even more different. As Breathnach says, "Traditional players are not, in any event, obsessed with the bookish idea that there can be only one correct version of a tune."[19]

Don't be the least bit intimidated by this. This versatility is not nearly so difficult to acquire as it would seem, if approached systematically. However, for the student just starting out, the solution to this is to learn a part one way, that is, as it's played in a tune just the first time through for instance, and for purposes of building skills in a

---

[19] Breathnach, Breandán. *Folk Music and Dances of Ireland*, (1996). p. 120.

systematic fashion, learn only this one way of playing it for now. And the same goes for the B part; learn it as you hear it played one way, and for now learn just this one set form of the melody, repeating it over and over again in your mind, until you can hum the melody with relative ease, or at least something you feel is pretty close to it. Now you're ready to learn the tune on the whistle, in the old way, without recourse to reading the music. After all, as O'Neill says, "Neither harpers nor pipers made use of printed music even when available in the eighteenth and nineteenth centuries, as in fact, the majority of them were blind and of necessity obliged to learn and teach by the oral method only."[20]

The First Note

The first step is to find the correct first note. This is actually half the battle. Every melody, just like the modal scales I introduced you to in the first part of the book, is a sequence of notes, just the same. A melody can be played chromatically in any 'key' and still be the same melody, albeit at a higher or lower pitch, but a melody is in only one mode, and cannot be played in another mode without drastically altering the character of the melody. Most often tunes simply won't work in the wrong mode. So to learn a tune by ear, you must find the first note of the melodic sequence with trial and error, experimenting with the first few notes. Here, you'll see how the practice of the modal scales applies to getting tunes figured out. With some practice, this first step rapidly becomes quite automatic, but initially, it is the logical process of note-at-a-time analysis: does the second note sound higher or lower than the initial tone? How many tones above or below? Is the time value the same, that is, is the note held as long as, or longer, or for not as long a time? You'll know right away you've begun with the wrong note if within three or four notes of piecing together a melody, a step from one note to the next is a half-step when your ear wants to hear a whole step, or a whole step (up or down) when your ear is looking for a half-step. This simply means the incorrect first note has you started off in the wrong mode. Try another starting point until the sequence sounds correct. Remember, as many or more tunes will be using the G major framework as the D, so try both (in session playing, when experienced players hesitate, trying to remember how a tune starts, they often say they're looking for the first note.)

Now, of course you can look up the melody in sheet music, and find the first note, thereby referring back to the fingering charts, but by doing so, be aware that you'll short-circuit a sub-conscious learning process that proves a valuable tool in learning tunes later on (the process is, in part, the mind learning to recognize a melody's mode). We'll shortly be discussing how to memorize a tune you've never heard before from the written page, but if you turn your attention, even a small amount, to learning to read sheet music at this time in your development, you risk serious damage to your mind's ability to recall tunes without it. With training, a tune can easily be learned from a written page and remembered, but only after all mnemonic skills have been developed and are in place, and not before.

About Written Music

Let's talk a bit about written music. Music, vocal and instrumental, existed as an art long before any means to record it, in any place other than the memory. Music, as any composer knows, must be created in the imagination before it becomes a reality played upon an instrument, or symbols on a graph drawn out on paper. The graphic system we know as musical notation is a wonderful invention, and allowed the coherent synchronization necessary for larger ensembles, both vocal and instrumental, which, in turn, allowed the development of our modern polyphonic choral and symphonic music. But even the most skilled of the classical performers will acknowledge that in sight reading, they are only learning the melody, not *playing* it, that the notes on paper must become at least familiar before they can be played back with any feeling, that is, as *music*.

---

[20] O'Niell, Francis. ***Irish Minstrels and Musicians***, (1913). p. 126.

Let me mention a problem I had learning to read sheet music as a youth. As soon as I had played a piece of flute music for a few repetitions, reading from the written notation, I would begin to remember it, and upon a repeat try, would simply play back what I remembered, unfortunately letting my eyes wander enough to lose my place. On taking this problem to my teacher, Ralph, I received a very eloquent explanation of the real heart of the matter. Regarding reading the music, I just needed to work on my concentration; that's the way it always is learning. But of course, we don't really read the music after thorough rehearsal as much as remember the music, the whole piece, no matter how lengthy or complex. He told me that when they get up on stage to play a symphony, they've rehearsed it so well that the whole orchestra knows each and every note of the piece they're about to play perfectly, by heart, and if they don't, they've no business being up there, for the notes must be internalized and remembered to be heartfelt, and played musically. The pages of the manuscript they turn have become just a cue sheet. As an example, he cited the soloist for a concerto, who knows, with no score to read from, not only every note they are to play, but every note in the entire composition. This explanation made an indelible impression on me, and gave me a working understanding of what music really is as a performance art.

This being understood about written notation, I want to dissect a tune, written out in notation, to explain something of a system a lot of the tunes follows, as a further aid to recalling these 8-bar parts. This system is aptly described by Breandán Breathnach:

> With the exception of a score or so of tunes to which special dances are performed, all these tunes share a similar structure. Each consists of at least two strains or parts of eight bars – there are no dance tunes and only very few airs which only have one strain. In the vast majority of tunes, each part is made up of two phrases. The common pattern is a single phrase repeated with some slight modification, with the phrases falling naturally into half-phrases of two bars each. A basic element present alike in song and dance music is exhibited in these half-phrases; the first making, as it were, an assertion to which the second is the response. This principal of contrast is present to some extent even between the two phrases of a strain, although, as suggested, the melodic differences, if any, may be only slight.[21]

A tune that is a good example of this is #69 from ***O'Neill's Dance Music of Ireland***, "Philip O'Neill." Even if you do not yet read notation, the obvious similarities and differences will communicate the point to you.

Now, let's arrange the parts and bars this way:

---
[21] Breathnach, Breandán. *Folk Music and Dances of Ireland*, (1996). p. 56.

In the two bar 'half-phrases' of the first part, it's easy to see the first and third pair (the 'assertion') are so nearly identical as to be interchangeable:

In the second part, the first and third pair of bars are wholly identical, as are the last two bars of the first part, with the last two bars of the second part. So, in memorizing this two part jig, then, you've really only five individual two bar half-phrases to remember, each

Dye – del – dee Dye – del – dee Dye – del – dee Dye – del – dee

in length, and arranged so as to respond to each other's melodic pattern, really designed to memorize! This simplicity of form combined with a frank sentimental honesty is the hallmark of the Irish dance music.

Of course, you'll soon notice that, as well, many tunes seem to go the opposite direction altogether, with melodies odd and winding, as if doing their best to be as confusing as possible. These become memorable in their own fashion, but to return to the first point, remember that to pick a tune that's attractive to you is the main thing. The preceding analysis techniques should be of help with it, but no set formula will be applicable to all.

Developing Breathing Skills

Let's take an overview of where we've come to with all this.

If you are listening to the music and are finding tunes you like and are able to recall, if you've gained an essential understanding of how whistles work and are able to make tones – how to play all the notes of both octaves, hopefully, and are beginning to find the melodies out with experimentation, then, you are at the critical juncture, and lack only one key component to begin to play – the ability to breathe so as to keep a good rhythm.

The first step, of course, is to figure out the notes of your tune, getting all in place with the right proportionate time value to each. And the next step is to gain the ability to play the melody through and through again to a good, solid beat. There is an instrumental form known as the Slow Aire, which is played in a loose, arrhythmic style, which we will discuss later on, but one of the major, defining characteristics of the dance music is the dominating, solid, compelling rhythm, to which the melody is always subject. And here's where I want to discuss something I mentioned early on; how you won't be able to keep a rhythm at all until you learn how to breathe. Now that you know the notes of the whistle, now that you have a tune in mind with a melody you can recall and *hum through complete*, and can find all the notes for the tune, no matter how clumsily or slowly, now finally, you are at the point where you can meaningfully learn how to breathe as you play, or rather, play as you breathe.

The truth is, it doesn't take that much air to play the whistle. What happens when you take a large breathful and play a long string of notes is the air in your lungs will be depleted of oxygen before you've run out of steam for blowing notes, which creates a gasping effect, causing the beginner to pant to try to recover necessary oxygen and breaking down control. This thing of breathing is really the last hurdle before being able to play a tune solidly through, at which point you can finally begin in earnest, learning ornamentation and tunes and giving them your own interpretation. And now that you know a tune, you can use it as a tool to learn to breathe. With a straightforward approach, it's not hard to learn.

If you've looked into other whistle books, you may have seen where some will show you sheet music with little symbols drawn in, "breathe here." This is often counter-productive, as the beginner too often instinctively plays up to the symbol, stops for breath, and then continues, *still prioritizing getting all the correct notes in at the expense of a constant rhythm*. You are much better off with no other guide than your breathing reflexes. The secret to learning to breathe and play with steady rhythm is in this step-by-step process: learn all the notes to a tune so you know where they go well, but once that's accomplished, make attempting to play in a steady rhythm the priority, dropping as many notes as you need to keep a beat, however slow. The notes you drop, however many, while initially struggling through a tune to a regular beat, will rapidly be able to be 'picked up' again later on, but by putting all emphasis on keeping rhythm rather than playing all the correct notes at this juncture in your learning curve, you force yourself to adapt a way to manage the breath as part of the ongoing melody. The body has to intuit this on its own, as your reflexes for oxygen are the driving factor here, spontaneous and natural.

Don't fill your lungs way up, but instead take small and frequent breaths; this keeps adequate oxygen to the brain and muscles as well as helping you develop a way to pull in quick, small breaths 'in time.' Repetition is the tool to build strength here – once you can finish a tune through to a steady beat and repeat it through again, keep going! Play the tune in a circle, A-A B-B A-A B-B A-A B-B as best you can as long as you can. Much more than learning the tune here *you are learning to breathe as you play*. The same type of dip in the learning curve may occur as with initially learning smooth finger movement, in that after the first success at keeping a rhythm, it may elude you again as your body intuits a way to accommodate this unique demand, which generally occurs much too quickly for conscious thought processes. But like swimming (perhaps a lot), stay in the water, that is, play this first tune you've learned the notes to over and over and again and again nonstop as long as you can and in very little time the process of breathing as you play will become so natural as to be completely spontaneous. I found taking this general approach to learning efficient breathing skills much more effective than a tune-by-tune approach.

Breathing, studied by repetitively playing a tune for minutes on end, if possible, will in no time build spontaneous, eloquent breathing skills requiring no more thought than the breath required for speaking. But repetition is your tool here, and duration. Ask any wind instrument player, and they'll tell you; it's more than performing music. For us, it's also something of an aerobic exercise. Be tough on yourself here, and it will pay off with rapid progress.

While we're talking about rhythm, I would like to mention the metronome. Some people find them helpful, but I personally don't recommend them, as the imperative, machine-steady beat often confuses, causing the student to stop and start over, when what's desired is a steady non-stop cycle of repetitions. I think you're much better off keeping your own beat with a tap of the foot (your rhythm doesn't need to be perfect as you're learning to breathe, just *continuous*). This is really quite important, for in tapping your foot as you learn to breathe in time with your melody your whole body participates somewhat in getting your sense of rhythm to develop as you play. This is of fundamental importance as being dance music, if the steady beat is interrupted, the whole performance falls apart. Performance shows the priority; not many notice or care if you drop a few notes here and there, but a break in the tempo will be immediately recognized as far as your music carries. So cultivate a good sense of rhythm with a tap of the foot as you begin to get a tune up to a good solid rhythm, as this is a potent tool for making progress.

About Learning Tunes from Notation

At this point, I would like to discuss memorizing a tune you've never heard before from notation, that is, sheet music.

If you've been a disciplined student, and have acquired the mnemonic skills required to recall a melody after hearing it (albeit one hundred times), and can play the whistle with enough skill to play a handful of tunes with steady rhythm, you are at the point in your learning curve where written notation will possibly be more of an asset than a liability to your progress.

If, however, you notice that after acquainting yourself with written notation, you have more difficulty than before remembering melodies on your own, you should delay altogether or at least seriously reduce your study of written notation for the time being, for *if your mnemonic skills haven't developed to the point where you can remember what you've just heard yourself play from the page of notes, it not only does you no good whatsoever, but will also do a lot to arrest the development of your ability to recall tunes without it.*

As Ciaran Carson writes in his wonderful book ***Last Night's Fun***:

> It is possible, of course, to 'learn' a tune from the page, from what is there in black and white, but this requires negotiation and imagination. It requires you to know that what is written is a mere mnemonic, not an actual performance (it is impossible to transcribe an actual performance), nor the dynamic pulse of what it can be when it's played and heard and danced.[22]

Rather than detail how to read sheet music here, which so many books already do, let me instead continue with a description of how it is used.

Putting it in Your Fingers

Once you are able to piece together the notes of the first bar, or two bars at the most, stop. Play them again as best you can, stop. Can you recall in your mind what you just played? Can you hum it back to yourself? Do so as soon as you can, hum it again with the voice, and play it again, no matter how slowly, on the whistle *without looking at the page*. Work on these first two bars, playing them over and over until they make coherent sense to you. Keep your eyes off the written notes as much as you possibly can, referring to it only as necessary.

Step through the next segment (one or two bars) in the same fashion, leading into it from the part you're already acquainted with as best you can.

At four bars, half a part, is often the end of a melodic 'phrase,' give or take a lead-in note or two. As soon as any part of the melody has formed a recognizable syntax in your mind, repeat it over and over, humming it mentally, in your imagination, as best you can as you work through the notes on your whistle. This formula, when applied to learning a difficult passage of finger work slowly and then bringing it up to speed, is referred to as 'putting it in your fingers.' The mental humming in unison with the finger movements builds an automatic reflex (muscle memory) action associated with the melody as it is remembered, or you could say, as the tones are anticipated.

Continue on through the tune, making all the sense out of it that you can and repeating it back without looking at the written material as best you can. At first this process is slow and awkward, but with persistence it rapidly gains in ease, as again your sub-conscious mind assembles the necessary skills to accomplish this. Playing music usually happens at a tempo far too fast for typical thought processes, which, when they interject themselves, often stop the action altogether.

---

[22] Carson, Ciaran. ***Last Night's Fun***, (1996). p. 11.

Ornamentation

Here might be a good place to discuss ornamentation. You'll notice almost all the dance tunes as published in print are written out in a very simple and plain way, often without any ornamentation written in with it whatsoever. This is because, traditionally, all ornamentation and interpretation is wholly the musician's choice at time of performance, with no other influence than their imagination and current state of mind.

As O'Neill puts it, "…[A]mong traditional Irish musicians, nothing is so noticeable as the absence of uniformity of style or system."[23] As well, "To illustrate the wealth of graces, turns, and trills, which adorn the performance of capable Irish pipers and fiddlers, skillful both in execution and improvisation, is beyond the scope of exact musical notation."[24]

Some written music will suggest some, but it's really your game. This is where real musicianship develops.

Let me explain the technical aspects of how they're done, then we'll discuss an easy way to incorporate them into your playing.

Let me quote Breandán Breathnach on ornamentation:

> Irish folk music is essentially melodic. It uses no form of harmonic accompaniment or modulation, but relies for its effect on the ornamentation of the melodic line. Three main forms of ornamentation are employed: embellishment, variation, and rhythm. Examples of each type may be found in a single performance. Broadly speaking, however, the first or third may predominate because of the demands of the instrument being played or because it is a basic ingredient of a local style.[25]

What's meant by 'embellishment' of the melody is the addition of what are called grace notes, notes added in to accent those of the melody's basic structure. The ornaments most used on the whistle are called: pips, trills, turns (or rolls), and slurs (or slides).

The simplest, and one of the most profoundly affecting grace notes on the whistle is the pip, sometimes called the 'cut.' This consists of dropping to the note to be ornamented quickly from a note above. Quickly as in lightning speed, and typically from the note directly above the melody's note (as in B to A or A to G), but not necessarily, as for instance, piping an E note with a G. Try this: take a breath and hold an E note for a couple of seconds and while doing so, pop your G-note finger (the ring finger of your left hand) up and down in a flash. That's the sound of the pip – the sudden blip of an accenting note (any of the notes played with the right hand can be piped in this way). They're typically to initiate a 'quaver' of notes, or a 'phrase,' or anytime you're back into a phrase after pulling a quick breath. Pips are also a great way to accent a note that's sustained for a prolonged length of time.

The trill, as an ornament, is created by playing whatever note you want to trill, then the note above it (typically above, you can use the one below if you wish), back and forth lightning fast for the full time value of the note being trilled. In written music this is sometimes indicated by the letters Tr above the note to be trilled, sometimes by a wavy line drawn after the note. Trills, you'll find, don't work well with every melody, but are a great way to put some fire into, for instance, martial sounding jigs.

Remember – just because someone's sheet music calls for a trill doesn't mean that's what you must necessarily do, and just because it doesn't call for one doesn't mean you can't add one in if you think it sounds appropriate. To quote Breathnach again:

> When a printed text is used, as an aid to memory, in acquiring a group of notes which the ear refused to pick up, or later to add to one's repertoire, the text should not be regarded as sacrosanct, since *a*

---

[23] O'Neill, ***Irish Folk Music: A Fascinating Hobby***, (1910), p. 45.
[24] Carolan, Nicholas, ***A Harvest Saved: Francis O'Neill and Irish Music in Chicago***, (1997). p. 43.
[25] Breathnach, Breandán. ***Folk Music and Dances of Ireland***, (1996). p. 94.

*version of a tune acquires no particular validity by being committed to print…*When the tune has been added to one's repertoire, it should be regarded as one's own.[26]

Turns, or rolls, are a particularly beautiful ornament. As Ciaran Carson puts it so eloquently:

"To define a roll is difficult – it must be heard in order to be understood, or grasped. Basically, a roll consists of a five-step rhythmical cluster: you play the note to be rolled, then a note above the anchor note (the 'cut'), then the note, then a note below the note (the 'tip'), and finally the note gain. How you play the cut and the tip depends on whatever instrument you're playing, and how you want to emphasize or shape the roll; they consist of the merest flick of the fingers, and seem to exist outside of conventional time, since the quintuple movement happens in triplet time."[27]

A roll as an ornament works nicely anywhere a trill does, which seems to apply well to any note held relatively longer than the others in a tune; say a quarter note amongst quavers of eighth notes.

Drawn out on the musical staff, a roll looks like this:

Grace notes in sheet music are often drawn with miniature notes, so as to imply that they are grace notes, and not the actual melody. And like the man says, quickly, "a mere flick of the fingers."

The slur, or slide, is a particularly easy and effective ornament, a great way to draw that "high lonesome sound" out of your melody.

As the holes of the whistle are covered with the pad of the finger and not the tip, the slide is best accomplished by pushing the finger in a forward movement up and off the hole, rather than pulling it back towards the palm. By pushing the finger pad forward over, up and off the hole, better control of the airstream is maintained. In this way, the slur can be played slowly and deliberately for a Slow Aire, or quickly, yet articulately in a fast paced performance.

Try this: cover all holes but the bottom two, for a low F♯ note. Play a long, steady F♯ and as you do, push your right hand index finger forward, up and off the hole with a smooth, even movement, so only the top three holes are covered by the fingers of the left hand, for a G note (you'll notice slides work only in an upward direction).

Now try it with two notes at once. Cover all the holes but the bottom one for a low E note, and holding this low E, slide both the middle and index fingers forward at once, leaving the left hand holes covered for a slide from E up to G.

With a little practice, the technical aspects of playing these ornaments are easily mastered; but when to use them, how to work them into your melody?

There are two tools for learning ornamentation that are applied together; the slow aire, and the sound model. First, let me describe the slow aire, and then explain what I mean by sound model and how it applies.

---

[26] *Ibid.*, p. 123.
[27] Carson, Ciaran, ***Last Night's Fun***, (1996). p. 55.

The Slow Aire

The slow aire is a type of instrumental music, not of the dance category, but played in a very freestyle fashion, as a vocal aire is performed. The term 'aire' in its general application simply refers to a melody. Some have it that the term 'aire' refers to the melody of a song, while the term 'tune' refers to the melody of an instrumental dance piece.

What the term 'slow aire' means to an instrumentalist is that the tune is to be played very slowly and deliberately, in a pronounced song-like way, with as much expression, pure emotion and verve as the performer can deliver. Melodies in the slow aire form defy accurate rendition in written notation, for though the notes can be written in the right place on the staff lines the time values can only be suggested, and often defy 'barring' altogether.

A lot of dance melodies can be rendered in a slow aire style; practically speaking, as we first learn a melody on our whistle, piecing together the notes one sequence at a time, building up to one phrase at a time, we're playing the melody in a sort of slow aire style, that is; slowly and with all emphasis on playing the correct notes rather than keeping a beat. *This is the way to learn to ornament melodies as well.* Once you understand the melody, play it as a slow aire, drawn out and expressive, and try to give every phrase of notes an ornament of some kind; a pip, turn, trill or slide, and each time through see if you can use a different ornament than you did for the same notes previously. This is a much more effective way to learn ornamentation than to get a tune up to a solid beat and then try to force fit ornaments in at tempo pace. If you learn to play ornaments by playing melodies slowly and somewhat arrhythmically, with all focus on expressionate ornamentation, you're giving yourself not only a much better opportunity to learn, but a better opportunity to get a strong effect of feeling and grace, so this approach is very productive, the only requirement being patience.

The Sound Model

This is where what I call the sound model comes into play. At this point in your musicianship, you have to know what you want to sound like; that is, you have to have a model of how you want your tune to sound. This is where immersion in the music comes into play again. As you listen to the different recordings of the different musicians, exposing yourself to the eclectic range of styles and various renditions of tunes, just as certain tunes invariably will stand out as personal favorites for whatever reason, so as well will a particular style of playing them. And because this style of playing whatever tune by whomever the musician is what you find personally attractive, or beautiful, or somehow compelling, this becomes your sound model, that is, *what you will subconsciously if not consciously strive to model your sound after*. This is the way music has been learned from the beginning; we hear, and what we find beautiful or otherwise compelling, we try to emulate. This may have a lot to do with the development and evolution of local styles, in that musicians, if they hear a new way of playing that appeals, will automatically study it and adapt it as their own, which, by means of personal interpretation, does indeed become their own, another component of their own repertoire of effects.

To pick up Breathnach again where we left off:

> When the tune has been added to one's repertoire, it should be regarded as one's own. If another player has some touch or turn which appeals, there need be no hesitation about borrowing it. Imitating the style of some outstanding player is an excellent way of making progress in the initial stages of learning, but it is not a course one should persist in. As soon as some proficiency has been attained, one should listen to a tune to learn it, not to acquire its style. A second hand player always remains a second rate player.[28]

---

[28] Breathnach, Breandán. *Folk Music and Dances of Ireland*, (1996). p. 23.

Though obviously, for the beginner to be able to successfully copy a much admired artist is an indication of the progress you've accomplished, and does a lot to build confidence in your ability. You'll see, in future years, when you've learned to play fluently and have an eclectic repertoire in your memory, how easily and naturally your own style will develop. And this individual style will invariably be a mix of all the techniques and effects you yourself find attractive, effective, and compelling for whatever reason, that you learned from those musicians whose playing inspires you and helped you to create the valuable tool of your sound model!

Rhythmic Variation

Now, let's discuss ornamentation of the rhythmic variety. As we know, the solid beat of the dance music is an essential component of any performance, keeping the musicians together and giving the dancers their pace. Yet the emphasis on chosen melodic phrases can be dramatically manipulated by expanding or compressing the time value of the notes of the phrase, this being done without any change in the overall beat or tempo whatsoever. This comes much more easily to those who originally learn by ear as opposed to those who learn by reading notation, for, as Mr. Carson puts it, "They take the tune as read whilst a traditional musician plays the tune as heard."[29]

This aspect of ornamenting a tune clearly shows what is meant by O'Neill's quip about this music often being "beyond the scope of exact musical notation," though an example using the A part of the Mooncoin jig from ***The Music of Ireland*** (#1034) may serve to illustrate. Once again, this should make sense to the non-literate musician due to the visible difference in the graph.

Here, the last two bars of the first part played as written:

would suggest all the notes played with an even time value – an even beat of 1 – 2 – 3 – 1 – 2 – 3 – 1 – 2 – 3 – 1 – 2 – 3 per each quaver of three notes. This is obviously the most straightforward way to notate or play anything, one note per beat. However, the same two-bar phrase could be interpreted (that is, played) with the first note held longer for emphasis, and the following notes crammed into a run, all within the same steady beat, and ending on the high G note; which could be notated like this:

---

[29] Carson, Ciaran. ***Last Night's Fun***, (1996). p. 11.

This expanding of the A note's time and compressing of the rest into a 'run' gives the phrase a bright, martial sound, particularly if you stop abruptly on the high G note, with a lightning-fast, though noticeable gap in between the G as it moves to the F♯ note, and slightly compressing the last two.

Of course, a very pronounced effect is attained when the part is played in this fashion predominantly, and the last two bars played 'as written' as the exception instead, with emphasis on the pronounced evenness of the beat as the 'ornamentation'.

A technique known as 'tonguing' works well with this, creating what's called a 'staccato' effect. This is indicated in sheet music by a dot immediately above a note:

the opposite of

which indicates the 'legato' or smooth and flowing effect. This is done by initiating the tone with an abrupt burst of air created by touching the tip of the tongue to the roof of the mouth just behind the front teeth, and using it to release a sudden and unsustained blip of sound. This lends to a very crisp, sharp, choppy effect, giving the phrase a march-like, 'fife-and-drum' type feel that completely contrasts and wonderfully complements the aforementioned way of playing the phrase with the 'run.' It is in this way, by contrasting different types of ornamentation, that your tune can be artistically manipulated. As Miles Krassen succinctly phrases it, "...[P]articular flourishes are used judiciously over the course of a performance, rather than being crammed all together in one runthrough."[30]

Melodic Variation

This brings us to the other category mentioned by Breathnach, melodic variation. From his book, ***Folk Music and Dances of Ireland***:

> The second form of variation is an entirely different matter, involving as it does a degree of instant composition. Here the group or bar is varied, perhaps only the skeleton of the phrase being retained. Each time the part is played, some grouping is varied, no performance ever being the same. Two

---

[30] O'Neill Francis & Miles Krassen, *O'Neill's Music of Ireland: Revised and Corrected for Fiddle*, (2008), *Introduction*. p. 14.

players of the past come to mind in this connection: Michael Coleman, the fiddle player, and Johnny Doran, the piper. The ability to vary in this manner is a gift which, when combined with superior powers of execution, makes the supreme player, the virtuoso. It may be added that this is indeed a rare gift. The great majority of players who use variations of the kind in question have picked them up from other players or worked them out at their leisure. Memorized on the fingertips by practice, these variations automatically occur at the appropriate points, as do the simpler types in question above.[31]

The most common way I've heard these applied is in subtle note substitutions, omissions, or additions.

After playing the tune once through 'as learned,' or 'from the page,' or as generally recognized or whatever, the second time through subtle changes are introduced. As an example, let's use the tune "Top of Cork Road" from ***O'Neill's Dance Music of Ireland***."

The first four bars could also be played:

without altering anything of the essential character of the melody. It's still unquestionably "The Top of Cork Road" but with a few substitutions. The same four bars could be played:

which means the second note in the third bar is omitted altogether. The one beat gap this produces helps create a little bounce to the rendition as an ornament (note the new note substitutions in the fourth bar as well).

And there's the second part:

---

[31] Breathnach, Breandán. *Folk Music and Dances of Ireland*, (1996). p. 98.

where in the fourth bar the quarter note could be traded for a couple of eighth notes for an easy little change-up. These, in the idiom of Irish music, would be considered modest and subtle variations. Let's push another tune a little further:

This is a very popular old hornpipe made more interesting by its contested history. The first four bars I often hear played in this fashion:

As well the next four bars are easily altered; with an altogether different lead-in to the second part:

There's a variation I often hear in session playing that works well:

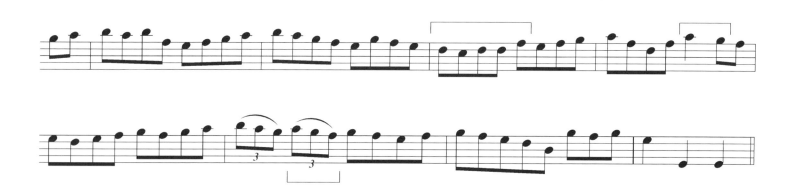

And this same tune is recorded in a dozen different ways in a dozen or more collections, and hence makes for a wonderful piece to study this with. No matter how it's played, it's still unmistakably "The Rights of Man," a very distinctive piece, easy to identify.

In playing around with melodies in this fashion, it is easy to see how new parts and multiple settings of tunes evolve. It is perfectly acceptable to borrow bars from different settings as you play your tune several times through, adding in your own changes, either planned or spontaneous, as you see fit. All this with a constantly changing array of ornament and rhythmic emphasis, over a steady, often driving, dancer's pace.

This, however, poses a question: doesn't this make ensemble playing a little chaotic, if not impossible? Chaotic, possibly, but certainly not impossible. The best sessions are often those in which there aren't too many of any one instrument, rather, one of each type is often more workable, as the differences in timbre of the various instruments mellows the possible clash of ornamentation occurring in the same musical phrases simultaneously. The model of performance, whether it be in a group, with a simple accompaniment or solo is still based wholly upon individual interpretation and expression.

As Breathnach puts it, "Traditional playing, it must be remembered, is of its very nature a personal expression, and the restraint demanded in playing in a band or other ensemble kills the spirit which animates it."[32]

However true this may be, there are few ways to improve your musicianship better than playing with a few friends. My recommendation is as soon as you have even a handful of tunes that you can play through a couple of times with a solid beat, find a friend with a fiddle, accordion, guitar – anyone really – who can play some tunes, and sit down and do so. Remember, this music was meant to be played, so don't be shy. The more discipline and energy you invest in it, the greater will be the payoff in skill and enjoyment. And I hope your payoff is great indeed!

Traditional music is saved by collectors, great and small, only in the sense that butterflies are collected and saved by entomologists. Its continuity as a living thing depends on those of us who play it and upon those of us who learn it. Its future rests in our own hands.[33]

– Breathnach, Breandán

---

[32] Breathnach, Breandán. *Folk Music and Dances of Ireland*, (1996). p. 122.
[33] *Ibid.*, p. 127.

Appendix 1

Strange Keys and Half-holing; Tunable Whistles

Most printed collections of jigs and reels render the notation in our amenable keys of one or two sharps. However, some older ones, including O'Neill's, will have tunes written in other keys. Some instructional whistle books show a method called "half-holing," covering half a hole in an attempt to make a chromatic half-step. It would follow that the extra sharps or flats required by the different notation would be possible in this fashion. That is not the case. Again, here's master piper and whistler Breanda'n Breathnach on the subject:

> Theoretically, all semitones can be obtained on the whistle by forking or arching the finger so that half of the appropriate hole is uncovered. This method is not commonly adopted by traditional players, as it is scarcely practicable when playing rapid dance music.[34]

Instead, the tune is better transposed to a workable key. An outstanding collection published by Miles Krassen, **O'Neill's Music of Ireland; Over 1000 Fiddle Tunes; a Newly Revised and Corrected Collection of the Dance Music of Ireland**, has many of these tunes transposed into the session player's keys.

However, don't let the key signature of three sharps dismay you. This is the key of A, which asks for a G sharp to be in the 'major' key, or Ionian mode. Try the tune without the G sharp, which simply pushes the tune from Ionian to Mixolydian mode, as this may sound fine, and could even be a more authentic modal rendition. In O'Neill's time, the piano had achieved an imperious popularity, and what wasn't played on, or at least accompanied by the piano, simply wasn't taken seriously, in the same way that in our time, if things are not done in computer format, they are automatically relegated to the back drawer. This had the effect of chromaticizing a lot of the music, by pushing it into an idiom that served more the fads of the moment than the traditions of old, and tunes being copied in odd keys was one result.

As well, I wish to say that the G can be sharped, or rather the A flatted, by bringing the ring finger of the left hand very close to, but not into contact with, the G hole. Give it a try; play the A note (either octave) and as you do, slowly bring your left hand ring finger close to the G hole, and back away again. Feel the air stream on your finger as you hear the tone bend? This makes for a good ornament, but no more than that. Any time spent practicing half-holing should be considered a possibly damaging waste of time.

I'd like to say a word about tunable whistles here. They will have a fipple piece that slides, thereby elongating the overall distance between the fipple blade and the bottom of the tube. It's been my experience that most whistles off the shelf are in fine tune really, any discrepancy in true pitch being more the result of an unsteady force of breath than any problem with the whistle. As well, the elongation of the distance from fipple blade to tube end only distorts the ratio of the other hole placements, and I don't think that helps matters much.

My recommendation is don't worry about your whistle being in 'tune,' just play a tune; you'll get it worked out. If you have a whistle that's just plain dissatisfactory, well, sell off some stock or real estate and go get another one.

---

[34] Breathnach, Breandán. *Folk Music and Dances of Ireland*, (1996). p. 83.

Appendix 2

The First Two Pages of Hornpipes From O'Neill's Dance Music of Ireland

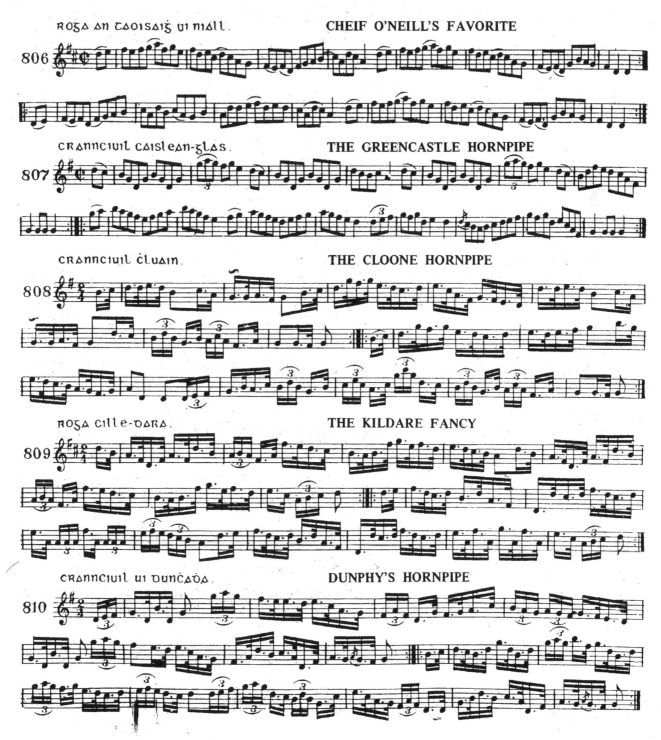

Appendix 3

Some Pointers on Reading Notation

Though I recommend the avoidance of sheet music for a considerable time while initially learning this music, there are a couple of simple counting drills I'd like to mention that aid in interpreting it.

When you see 16th notes (two flags) leading to eighth notes (one flag), think of it as *"and a,"* as in

And a 1 2 3 1 2 3 1 2 3 1 2 *and a* 1 2 3 1 2 3

Here is a good way to learn to assimilate triplets into your playing, which in notation are the notes grouped in threes with a joining crescent mark topped by the number three.

These three notes are to receive the same time value as one beat. A clever way to adjust to this count is to work it into a grid of numbers, spoken out loud in a rhythmical count, to an even tap of the foot.

Count:

111	2	3	4
1	222	3	4
1	2	333	4
1	2	3	444
111	2	3	4
1	222	3	4
1	2	333	4
1	2	3	444

This has been an effective tool for many in learning how to fit these into your playing.

Appendix 4

References and Recommended Reading

The Dance Music of Ireland: 1001 Gems Collected and Selected from All Available Sources and Edited by Capt. Francis O'Neill. (1907).

Walker, Ernest, ***A History of Music in England***, Oxford University Press, (1907).

Krassen, Miles, ***O'Neill's Music of Ireland, New and Revised***, Oakd Publications (1976).

North, Roger, and Hilda Andrews. ***The Musicall Grammarian***. London: Oxford University Press. (1725).

O'Neill, Francis, ***Chief O'Neill's Sketchy Recollections of an Eventful Life in Chicago***, Northwestern University Press (2008).

O'hAllmhur'ain, Gearo'id, ***A Pocket History of Traditional Irish Music***, The O'Brien Press (1998).

Shuter, Rosamund, ***The Psychology of Musical Ability***. Methuen & Co. Ltd. (1968).

The following referenced books are highly recommended:

Breathnach, Breanda'n, ***Folk Music and Dances of Ireland: A Comprehensive Study Examining the Basic Elements of Irish Folk Music and Dance Traditions***, Ossian Press Publications Co. Lt. (1996).

O'Neill, Capt. Francis, ***Irish Folk Music, a Fascinating Hobby***, Norwood Editions (1910).

O'Neill, Capt. Francis, ***Irish Minstrels and Musicians with Numerous Dissertations on related Subjects***, the Regan Printing House 1913 Reprint the Moxon Press (1987).

Carson, Ciaran, ***Last Night's Fun: In and Out of Time with Irish Music***, North Point Press (1996).

Carolan, Nicholas, ***A Harvest Saved: Francis O'Neill and Irish Music in Chicago***, Ossian Publications (1997).

Appendix 5

Furthering Your Musicianship and Sessions

It is a good habit to keep a log book of your practice time, perhaps what you worked on as well. This seemed to help me keep advancing in an organized fashion.

Keep a list of the tunes you learn, as well as a list of the ones you're interested in learning. It's surprising how quickly a tune can slip your mind; you can recall a tune from the mention of a name, but altogether forget its existence until reminded by the name. Break your list into two categories: tunes you know well, and tunes you're working on. As you continue to find new tunes, don't let those that have become familiar gather too much dust, as the repetitive playing of tunes you're already solid with never ceases to build strength of performance and increase the skill and versatility of your ornamentation.

I mentioned earlier playing music with a friend; the benefits of this can be multiplied greatly by going to a beach, park or some other public space. For practicing scales and initially figuring out tunes, it's nice to have a sense of privacy, but sooner or later, you're going to have to get used to the idea that when you're playing music with people, other people will be listening; for instance other people in a session, and the people in the pub, though they're probably busy with their own concerns. And nothing helps get a beginning musician past that initial shyness better than playing in a public place with a few people around who have other business altogether and really couldn't care less if you sound any good or not.

The most common reaction we get is one of interest and enthusiasm anyway, from those who don't ignore us altogether. This goes as well for busking, which is the term for street performing (Ireland has buskers' festivals). Truth, nothing will further your musicianship as well as this; for even the casual situation of playing on the curb for the passersby will do a lot to build the initiative required for session playing. Buskers traditionally play for tips, so a hat can be thrown down as an excuse for being there, if nothing else. Here you'll find what kind of musical effect you can really create, and the perfect laboratory for studying the epitome of the art, the solo performance.

Societal attitudes change rapidly over time towards "street music," and speak eloquently of the society's true character. In England, ca. 1725, Roger North (attorney general to King James II)[35] described how the attitudes towards music changed after the advent of the paid performance and the coming of the Italian opera. Merry old England, a land of extraordinarily rich musical culture (Tallis, Dunstable, Byrd, Purcell), suddenly was blighted with "…an ostentatious pride (that) hath taken Apollo's chair and almost subverted his monarchy."[36]

According to North, in the time of England's Civil Wars (1642-48), "…many chose rather to fiddle at home, than to go out and be knocked on ye head abroad;" now they paid to hear others perform for them instead, and a nation of fun-loving musical amateurs was suddenly made self-conscious.[37][38]

Turn of the century America, Capt. O'Neill's day, was soon to see the swing era, Jazz, and a modernity that overshadowed and disparaged the music brought over from the old countries, and many new immigrants themselves (including the Irish) all too willingly abandoned their traditional music with a strange and sudden shame.

---

[35] King James II was deposed in 1689

[36] North, Roger. *The Music Grammarian*, (1725). p. 41.

[37] *Ibid.*, p. 19.

[38] "To proceed now historically, we shall fall in with the reign of Charles I of which the first 10 years, that is, till ye Divell Incarnate confounded ye publick with his civill warrs, wealth, reputation, and arts, flourished more than ever was knowne before, or since, or is hoped forever to be knowne hereafter. And amongst other Arts, musick flourished, & exceedingly improved, for the King being a vertuous prince loved an entertainment as commendable as that was, And the fantazia manner held thro his reigne & during ye troubles & when most other good arts languished, musick held up her head, not at Court nor (in ye cant of those times) profane theatres, but in private society, for many chose rather to fidle at home, then to goe out & be knockt on ye head abroad; and the enterteinem was very much courted and made use of not only In country but citty familys, in which many of the Ladies were good consortiers and in this state was musick dayly Improving more or less till the time of (in all other respects But musick) the happy restauration." North, Roger. *The Musical Grammarian*, (1725). p. 18-19.

The beat era of the 1950s and '60s did a lot to shake loose people's apprehension about 'folk art'; by the hippie era of the '60s, the guitar-wielding troubadour, replete with ballads both old and new, had fortunately become a common part of American life. The post-hippie reaction of the yuppie era, however, has been to do its best to stifle that which is uniquely human and instead to promote a corporate sameness and conformity, safe within the bounds of mediocrity. So to go out busking then, is to take liege with Apollo, and defy our nation's current obsession with conformity and fear of criticism, instead encouraging individuality and art.

After a few times out busking, you may not feel like it, but you will be ready to go find a session group. Inquire at an (actual) Irish pub, most large cities have a few; if they don't sponsor one themselves, they might know one that does. The best session groups are informal and democratic; there may be a host to keep order, but each player takes a turn around the circle starting out the medley, calling both the tunes and setting the tempo. Some sessions will have a host that calls all the tunes, anyone else can fall in if they know it; but this is not nearly as fun.

The worst sessions will be a group of unwelcoming snobs, convinced of their superiority and emanating the aforementioned "ostentatious pride." O'Neill, in his writings, exhibits a large disdain for these types:

> Instead of the aid and encouragement, which talented novices have a right to expect from Irish musicians of mature years and more or less prominence, who loudly bewail the decline of Irish music, they are unfortunately treated with indifference if not open hostility as possible rivals. In their little fools' paradise of self-conceived superiority, most self-taught or untaught Irish pipers and fiddlers look with disdain – nay, even scorn, on aspiring students of Irish music who have had a modern musical education.[39]

These same types of sessions also have a tendency to play everything at breakneck speed. Now, everyone learns a tune at their own particular tempo, and in session playing, if a tune you're good with is being played slower than you're used to, there's a tendency to want to speed it up to the pace you're more familiar with. Be aware of this and restrain yourself – not only is it impolite, but often the medley will keep accelerating until the musicality is quite destroyed.

Here is O'Neill on the subject of tempo:

> Few musicians of any nationality find difficulty in playing Irish airs, but many appear to have little conception of that peculiar rhythm or swing without which Irish dance tunes lose their charm and spirit. We cannot justly criticize others for shortcomings in this respect when musicians of more than local repute, of Irish birth or ancestry, give public exhibitions of frenzied execution in dance music inconceivably beyond the capacity of the most expert dancer. The jig and reel, at their hands, become a mere jumble of sounds, disappointing to the ear and disqualified for the dancer. No Irish music, as played in Ireland or elsewhere, for the skillful Irish dancer, is livelier than quickstep time. Such favorites, for instance, as "Garryowen" and "Rory O'Moore" served equally well as jigs or marches. The prestige of Irish music has suffered an incalculable loss by disregard of the old Irish time, by many of its admirers and would-be friends, who no doubt obtained their erroneous ideas from the frantic contortions of vaudeville entertainers. Irish dance music was intended for Irish dancers, and neither the fancies nor the vagaries of musicians, humble or famous, will justify any faster time than a dancer requires. In deploring the decline of the once renowned music of Ireland, no reflection on the music of other countries is intended. To paraphrase a saying concerning a certain cheering beverage, 'All music is good, but some music is better.'[40]

---

[39] O'Neill, Francis, *Irish Folk Music: A Fascinating Hobby*, (1910). p. 275-76.
[40] *Ibid.*, p. 291-92.

Acknowledgements

A mountain of gratitude to Leslie Olsen, without whose efforts this might never have seen publication, as well as Nicole Jekich for lending her time and artistic skills to create the images featured in this book and also for taking the book to its completion.

Special Thanks To:

Dr.'s John and Julie Gottman for their enthusiasm and support.

Susan O. McClain for showing me the right direction.

And most of all to my mother, Arla W. Lebens, for passing on to me her love of fine music.

"Gentlemen—I conceive it to be the duty of every educated person closely to watch and study the time in which he lives, and, as far as in him lies, to add his humble mite of individual exertion to further the accomplishment of what he believes providence to have ordained."

– Prince Albert, ca 1850

About the Author

Stuart Esson is a carpenter and whistle tutor, who lives in Seattle, Washington.